Road Warriors

AP/Wide World

TRIUMPH
BOOKS

NEW YORK POST

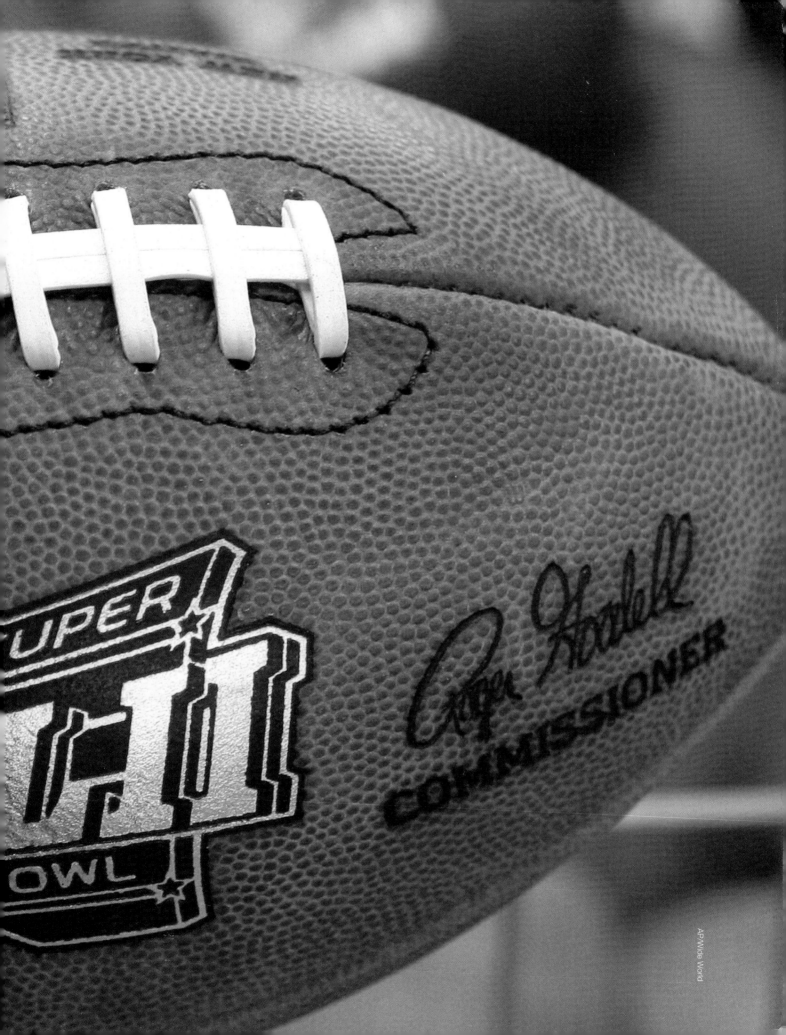

No part of this publication may be reproduced, stored in a retrieval system,
or transmitted, in any form by any means, electronic, mechanical, photocopying, or otherwise,
without prior written permission of the publisher, Triumph Books, 542 South Dearborn Street,
Suite 750, Chicago, Illinois 60605.

Triumph Books and colophon are registered
trademarks of Random House, Inc.

Content packaged by Mojo Media, Inc.
Joe Funk: Editor
Jason Hinman: Creative Director

This book is available in quantity at special discounts for your group
or organization. For further information, contact:

Triumph Books
542 South Dearborn Street
Suite 750
Chicago, Illinois 60605
(312) 939-3330
Fax (312) 663-3557

Printed in United States of America
ISBN: 978-1-60078-151-3

Photos courtesy of New York Post except where otherwise noted.

Contents

Introduction

By Mike Vaccaro

At the end, it was perfect that the final chapter occurred in the desert, where the faithful could wonder forever if it was all a mirage, because you could well spend the rest of your life as a New York sports fan and not enjoy the kind of ride the Giants put you on across the past six months.

That is the most remarkable thing about this, and about how easily the words—"New York Giants, Super Bowl XLII Champions"—roll off the tongue. That is the thing that allows you to keep coming back as a sports fan. The possibilities that every season bring. The dreams they foster. And the joy they yield.

The Giants started the season by getting rolled over in Dallas.

They were blown out at home by Green Bay. They trailed the Redskins 17-3 at the half in Week 3, and Washington was set up first-and-goal at the 1 at the end of that game, and the Giants were within a whisker of going 0-3, and the season would have been over before it began.

But the Giants held on. They held the line. They kept the Redskins out of the end zone, and by the time they got back to the visitor's locker room at FedEx Field that afternoon they were able to look around at each other and think: maybe we really do have something. Maybe we really can be special.

"I don't know that anyone believed at that moment that we were going to win the Super Bowl, necessarily," Michael Strahan said. "But I think we did realize that we were going to win some football games. And once you start to feel that way there isn't much of a stretch between that and what else you're capable of doing."

Even as they piled up wins, there were questions. Even as Eli Manning, the quarterback, began collecting feel-good moments, he seemed bent on balancing them out with moments, and with games, that would make you shake your head in wonderment and in anger. The defense had its spasms of collapse. The offense could look inert. You could hear the mutterings, about how this was a cosmetic record compiled by an unworthy team. You heard that a lot, in fact.

Only something happened just before the New Year.

First, the Giants overcame a 14-0 deficit in the swirling winds and angry snows of Buffalo two days before Christmas, wrapping up a playoff berth and allowing them to treat their coach, Tom Coughlin, to a frigid Gatorade shower. Then, with nothing to play for six days later, with the 15-0 Pats in town and the Giants' place in the playoffs secure, Coughlin made a fateful decision.

"We're gonna play to win," he announced to his team early that week. He reiterated it on game day, and repeated it one more time when the Giants returned to the locker room at halftime, leading 21-16. The lead would swell to 12, 28-16, and the Giants would still be leading entering the fourth quarter. That they would

lose, 38-35, seems almost incidental now, doesn't it?

Because that was really what started the Giants' real season.

"We were angry that we lost," Amani Toomer, the only other remaining member (besides Strahan) of the Giants' previous Super Bowl team, said. "Everyone wanted to compliment us on a job well done, but we knew we hadn't done what we wanted to do. We wanted to win the thing."

Amazingly, astoundingly, astonishingly, they would get that chance.

They would go on the road to Tampa and they would dominate the Buccaneers. They would go on the road to Dallas and they would hold off the Cowboys. They would go on the road to Green Bay—to the very frozen tundra itself, Lambeau Field, where it was 23 below with

Michael Strahan reacts while answering a question about the gap in his teeth during a media session the week before Super Bowl XLII.

the wind chill—and hold off the Packers.

And then they would come to suburban Phoenix, to this odd-looking dome in Glendale, and they would turn 18-0 into 18-1, they would look the Pats in the eye, same as they did in December, and this time it would be the Pats who would blink, the Pats whose defense would buckle, the Pats whose star-spangled offense would come up lacking when they needed as many points as possible.

A mirage in the desert, the Giants beating the Patriots.

Only this time, the mirage turned out to be a miracle. It turned out to be the real thing. ■

Preseason • August 11, 2007
Giants 21 • Panthers 24

Giant Holes Exposed In Big Blue D

No Stop In 'Em By Steve Serby

Collect call from Michael Strahan . . . No, Giants GM Jerry Reese isn't ready to accept any such call from his marquee holdout. But this couldn't possible have been the start Tom Coughlin and new defensive coordinator Steve Spagnuolo envisioned.

Big Bad Blue.

"We didn't look very good even though this was our first preseason game," Osi Umenyiora said as the Giants lost 24-21 to the Panthers last night. "We've got a lot of work to do. They got a couple of big runs on us, a couple of cutbacks on us, and that's not good. We have to get a lot better. This is the first preseason game, and we didn't really know what they were going to do because you don't gameplan much and we just came out here and played football, but again we have to do much better."

On his opening series, Jake Delhomme (5-for-8, 30 yards, 1 TD) converted a pair of third downs with short passes before DeShaun Foster cutback to his left and bulldozed Sam Madison, who returned to orbit to make the tackle after a 15-yard gain. Then, with new strongside linebacker Mathias Kiwanuka sucked inside, Nick Goings raced around right end for 21 yards, to the 6, before Delhomme found Steve Smith for the 5-yard TD pass against Madison that made it 7-0.

"Things didn't go the way we wanted it to," Antonio Pierce said. "Opening up the preseason by letting the other team score a touchdown on their first drive is not good. We've got a lot of work to do. We are still learning this new defense, but that's no excuse."

A 67-yard kickoff return by Derrick Ward set Eli Manning up at the Carolina 25. On third-and-9, out of the shotgun, Manning hit Sinorice Moss, who turned the underneath dumpoff into a 10-yard gain. Brandon Jacobs (4-15) powered for seven yards and on third-and-3, Manning (3-for-5, 27 yards, 1 TD in two series) scrambled up and found a lane and sidearmed one low over the middle to Jeremy Shockey for a 7-yard TD that tied it. "I was going to run and then I saw Shockey coming back to the ball," Manning said.

Carr got an interference call against Kevin Dockery then hit Ryne Robinson on a slant for 17 yards before Goings raced around left end on third-and-9 for 11 yards. From the 6, Big Blue forced John Kasay to settle for a 24-yard field goal.

Jared Lorenzen, third-and-6, found special- teams ace David Tyree, fighting for a roster spot, for 18 yards then, fourth-and-5 from the Carolina 38, executed a pretty screen pass to Reuben Droughns, who used a crisp block from Guy Whimper to rampage for 32 yards.

On third-and-5, Ward used a block from tight end

(opposite) Eli Manning did some scrambling in the preseason opener against Carolina.

AP/Wide World

Darcy Johnson to burst up the middle on a draw for the touchdown that gave the Giants a 14-10 lead.

Carr took over at his 27 with 48 seconds left in the half and Big Blue surrendered an inexcusable touchdown.

Safety Craig Dahl hit a defenseless Chris Horn following an incompletion and was flagged for 15 yards. Then Carr found Robinson for 24 yards, and out of bounds. Carr found Taye Biddle wide open with a 23-yard TD pass with seven seconds left because Corey Webster decided to zig inside when he should have zagged.

"I made the point at the half that we're not thin-skinned," Coughlin said. "You make mistakes and you rise up and do something about it in the second half. . . . I saw

(above) Sam Madison hangs on by a shoestring to make the tackle. (opposite) Despite the Giants' best defensive efforts, they would fall short in the preseason opener.

a lot of positives. The tackling is not one of them, but we did some good things with our kickoff return team."

In one earhole, out the other. Brett Basanez found Biddle with an 85-yard TD strike past Dockery at the start of the third quarter to make it 24-14.

J-Load hit Anthony Mix with a 10-yard TD pass to make it 24-21.

Anthony Wright was unable to engineer a scoring drive in the fourth quarter. ■

AP/Wide World

Preseason • August 19, 2007
Giants 13 • Ravens 12

Black And Blue

Giants Topple Ravens, But Lose Four To Injury By Paul Schwartz

The Giants last night did not abide by the first rule of the preseason—stay healthy—in their 13-12 victory over the Ravens at M&T Bank Stadium.

This for a time appeared to be a devastating evening for the Giants. Before the second quarter was more than just a few minutes old, starters and key reserves could be seen either limping off the field or getting carted off. In a span of 2:17 in actual clock time, four players went down. Receiver Michael Jennings is done for the season with a ruptured left Achilles tendon, safety Will Demps (dislocated elbow) figures to be out several weeks and cornerback Sam Madison (hamstring) and rookie receiver Steve Smith (concussion) could not finish the game.

Smith was hurt hauling in the game's lone touchdown, a 10-yard scoring pass from Eli Manning (10 of 13, 114 yards), who was solid despite getting sacked twice and losing the ball once on a fumble. Josh Huston helped his cause with a 50-yard field goal early in the fourth quarter and a 30-yarder with 5:57 remaining.

The Giants defense, so shabby in the preseason opener, clearly was more inspired. Willis McGahee was stopped cold (six rushing attempts, three yards) and the Ravens failed to score a touchdown. The one glaring negative for the Giants was 12 penalties.

There's a strong possibility that help is on the way. Sources said defensive end Michael Strahan is likely to end his holdout—which has reached 24 days—and return to the Giants. He is not expected to report to Albany this week, meaning he will miss the entire monthlong training camp. The Giants break camp Thursday. General manager Jerry Reese yesterday met with Strahan's agent, Baltimore-based Tony Agnone, at the team hotel and Agnone informed Reese that Strahan is nearing a decision.

It is possible Strahan will be on the scene Saturday night at Giants Stadium when the Giants face the Jets. There is no way Strahan can be ready to play in that game, though he has been working out in the Los Angeles area. He possibly could be available for the August 30 preseason finale at New England.

An NBC report, however, said Strahan's family is trying to convince him to retire.

Without Strahan, the starting defense showed significant improvement from its dismal preseason debut. On the first play, linebacker Mathias Kiwanuka shed a block by tight end Todd Heap to drop McGahee for a five-yard loss. Early in the second quarter, defensive tackle Barry Cofield surged in to nail McGahee for a four-yard loss.

Though they led 7-3 early in the second quarter, the Giants were battered. Jennings started in place of Plaxico Burress and played well with three receptions for 33 yards. On his final catch, an 11-yarder stretching near the right sideline early in the second quarter, Jennings

(opposite) Eli Manning pivots to hand off against the Ravens.

AP/Wide World

(above) Manning went down for a sack, but managed to escape injury. (opposite) Brandon Jacobs powers through would-be tacklers.

stepped awkwardly and limped off with a ruptured left Achilles tendon, ending his season.

"He was improving by leaps and bounds," coach Tom Coughlin said.

"I wish this wouldn't have happened," Jennings said. "I'm just going to twinkle my gold teeth and smile. I will be back. Look for one-five, one-five will be back."

Two defensive backs, Madison and Demps, went down on the same play, a 12-yard completion to running back Musa Smith. Demps was the more serious, as he lowered his shoulder trying to tackle Smith and came away with a dislocated right elbow. He said it's the exact same injury he suffered six years ago as a rookie with the Ravens. It's normally a 4-to-6 week injury but Demps said he plans to be back in 2-to-3 weeks.

"It felt like my bone was out and they popped it back in place," Demps said. "It's a sight that people shouldn't see."

Madison, away from the ball, changed direction and went down and out with a pulled left hamstring. Last season, Madison missed four games with a strained right hamstring. ■

Preseason • August 25, 2007
Giants 12 • Jets 20

A Giant Start

Despite Loss, Big Blue Starters Dominate Jets By Paul Schwartz

The Giants dominated on the field but not on the scoreboard last night while their starters were in action against the Jets. It was a 12-6 Giants lead at halftime before the reserves finished up and faltered in a 20-12 preseason loss to the Jets at humid and sweaty Giants Stadium.

After the Jets struck suddenly for a 79-yard touchdown on the very first play, the Giants dominated the remainder of the first half, outgaining the Jets 201 to minus-13 in yardage. Playing the first half, Eli Manning (17 of 35, 146 yards, 1 TD) was solid but not especially productive.

"As an offense, we have to find a way to keep the ball alive and drive down there and get touchdowns," Manning said. "Coming into tonight, we knew the Jets had been a kind of 'bend but don't break' defense and that's exactly what happened."

On defense, the Giants figure to have Michael Strahan back this coming week, as he's finally expected to end his holdout. Without him, the starting defense last night had one monumental lapse and then was rock-solid. Running back Leon Washington breezed out of the backfield and when Chad Pennington pump-faked, cornerback R.W. McQuarters bit big-time, leaving Washington free on the right sideline. Not only did Washington make the catch, but he cut inside past lunging safety James Butler and was gone. One play, 79 yards, one touchdown, and a 6-0 Jets lead after Mike Nugent's extra point failed.

"I'm not sure exactly what happened on that first play, but it was ugly," linebacker Antonio Pierce said.

"The quarterback got me on the pump fake," McQuarters said. "I thought he was going to throw, so I tried to jump it, but I should have stayed down and fell back deep. It was just one of those things and I messed it up."

After that, the defense went seven consecutive series without allowing a first down and Strahan this week will be added to the mix.

"It's definitely a void missing without his experience and leadership," said defensive end Justin Tuck, who excelled filling in for Strahan with four tackles and one sack. "I expect to see him [today] but who knows with Stray. He's a man of surprises."

The Giants reserves could not muster a point after halftime and the second-team defense allowed 14 third-quarter points to allow the Jets to pull ahead. "Our second group has got to play better," Tom Coughlin said.

No one had a worse first half than Lawrence Tynes, acquired from the Chiefs and who by now was supposed to have nailed down the kicker job. Guess again.

Tynes missed field goals of 40 and 43 yards, the first wide right, the second wide left. On the second miss, the snap by rookie Jay Alford was low and holder Cory

(opposite) Manning got solid protection on this play, a trend that would carry over into the regular season.

AP/Wide World

Ohnesorge—filling in for Jeff Feagles (back spasms)—had to rush to place the ball down without the laces in the proper alignment. Tynes in the second quarter was able to hit a 40-yarder.

"It's not impossible, but it's tough," Tynes said of working with a new snapper and holder. "It's not a great situation but I don't have any excuses. I missed the kicks." Tynes' competition, Josh Huston, was impressive in sending a kickoff late in the second quarter sailing out of the end zone for a touchback. Huston, though, missed a 42-yard attempt in the fourth quarter.

A crisp two-minute drill engineered by Manning

(above) The Giants defense gangs up on a Jets back during fourth quarter action. (opposite) Brandon Jacobs gets upended, one of the few times all year one man was able to bring him down.

started with an 11-yard pass to first-year receiver Anthony Mix and ended with Manning tossing a fade into the right corner of the end zone—a pass usually thrown to Plaxico Burress. The 6-foot-5 Mix made like Burress, leaping over the reach of 5-10 cornerback Manny Collins for a 5-yard touchdown catch. Coughlin might as well inform Mix (7-45 in the first half) that he's won himself a roster spot. ■

AP/Wide World

Preseason • August 30, 2007
Giants 20 • Patriots 27

Big Blue Whew!

No Casualties As Giants Drop Final Tuneup By Paul Schwartz

The Giants got in and out of their final preseason game without incurring any significant injuries. They received some decent work from their starting units. They did not suffer any new injuries. They saw a few flashes from youngsters. And, most importantly, did we mention that nobody got hurt?

Given the way they've been battered and bruised this summer, the Giants last night had to be satisfied with getting out of Gillette Stadium in one piece, though they lost 27-20 to the Patriots to finish an uneven preseason 1-3.

"With this game, we did what we needed to do," linebacker Antonio Pierce said. "We did give up a field goal. The first unit did well with our series. Everyone came out healthy."

The one injury reported by the Giants was a sprained ankle by backup offensive tackle Guy Whimper. Other than that, they got out clean and are glad to be done with these practice games.

"I don't think so," said tight end Jeremy Shockey, when asked if he needed to play in this game. "But if you're asked to do it, you do it. It can't hurt." Pats coach Bill Belichick treated this game like a glorified scrimmage. Of the 22 Patriots starters, only fullback Heath Evans made his way onto the field.

Tom Coughlin wanted his own starters to get some work and thus it came as no surprise that Eli Manning (5 of 8, 58 yards) in his one possession of the night methodically ripped through the New England backups. Coughlin saw enough after Manning moved his team 80 yards in 16 plays, eating 8:13 off the clock.

Manning dusted off Shockey, who had just two catches coming into this game. Shockey (4-47) got to break a sweat and his 20-yard reception put the Giants on the New England 2-yard line. From there the Giants had difficulty pushing aside the Pats scrubs. Adding in a penalty, it took the Giants five plays to get in. After an incomplete pass and two no-gains for Brandon Jacobs, on fourth down Jacobs ran behind a block from Guy Whimper for the touchdown.

"I wish it hadn't taken us five plays to get in there, but we got in and got the seven points," Manning said. "That's what you want in your final preseason game. You want to come out and have one good drive, score a touchdown and come out."

Jacobs (8-21) finished the preseason with 29 rushing attempts and 102 yards but did not like how long it took the Giants to crack the goal line.

"I thought I ran well," Jacobs said. "Obviously the goal line series was a little shaky. It shouldn't have taken us that many snaps to get the ball in. We have to be better than that."

(opposite) With the defense all over him, Kevin Boss was unable to hold on to the pass.

AP/Wide World

The starting defense was not as crisp. Tom Brady looked great on the sideline wearing a baseball cap and his backup, Matt Cassel, managed to put together a field goal drive—after taking over on the New England 49-yard line late in the first quarter. The many injuries to the defensive unit meant coordinator Steve Spagnuolo could not make wholesale changes and for the remainder of the first half, the two starting safeties (Gibril Wilson, James Butler), cornerback R.W. McQuarters, and linebacker Mathias Kiwanuka remained on the field.

This was Kiwanuka's final tuneup making the transition from defensive end to strong side linebacker and he looked out of synch on one play, failing to drop in coverage quickly enough as tight end Marcellus Rivers got past

(above) This pass was just out of the reach of Anthony Mix. (opposite) Few could have predicted that a typically uneventful preseason game between the Giants and Patriots would be a prelude to their showdown in the Super Bowl.

him for an 18-yard catch.

"I feel good about where I am," Kiwanuka said of the position change. "I feel good about the progress I've made every step along the way. I always understood there would be some ups and downs. I understood it was going to be difficult and be a challenge and I would be tested, but I like where I am and I like how I have come out of the preseason: a better player. I definitely feel ready to line up against Dallas." ∎

Regular Season • September 9, 2007
Giants 35 • Cowboys 45

For Big Blue

Defense Truly Rests For Giants By Mike Vaccaro

The quarterback's right shoulder is a concern, because the quarterback's shoulder will always be a concern when it leaves a game bruised, when it departs a city a little less healthy than when it arrived.

So the Giants will hold their breath with Eli Manning this week, they'll see how the wing responds to ice and to treatment and they'll hope he'll be at full strength next week, when the Packers come to Giants Stadium for the home opener. As well as Manning played last night against the Cowboys, it's enough to make you wonder what the season holds in store for him.

But as poorly as the Giants' defense played last night, it's enough to make you want to shrug your shoulders—even bruised shoulders—and wonder something else:

What good will an ascendant Eli Manning be to the Giants if he can throw for 312 yards and four touchdowns and put 35 points on the board on the road . . . and still lose by 10?

"The Cowboys," defensive end Justin Tuck said, "definitely put a kink in our plans."

They kinked up the plans and they tore up the blueprints and they dented and chipped and splattered everything else wearing blue last night. This woeful night should best be remembered by four numbers, in ascending order of importance:

There is one (1), which is how many punts the Giants defense forced, which is almost hard to believe. There is 142, the number of yards the Cowboys gained on the ground, and 345, which is how much Tony Romo collected through the air. And, most shameful, there is 45. When you surrender 45 points on opening night, it doesn't often inspire happy harbingers of what's to come.

"Nothing went well for us," linebacker Antonio Pierce said. "And it's hard to win when you don't do anything well."

"We let the whole offense down," added safety Gibril Wilson, who did make the defense's one notable contribution, picking off a foolish Romo pass midway through the fourth quarter that temporarily offered an illusion of escape, which helped set the offense up to make it 38-35 with time left for a stop and a score.

And only made the resulting, game-clinching 51-yard scoring strike from Romo to Sam Hurd as much a coup de grace as a calamity.

"We just couldn't stop them," Tom Coughlin said.

Coughlin had better hope he didn't just provide the five-word epitaph for this season in Week 1, but until further notice it's impossible to think otherwise.

Maybe the Cowboys really are as explosive as they looked all across last night's 45-35 romp at Texas

(opposite) Still working into game shape, Jeremy Shockey had to stop and catch his breath during the second half.

Michael Strahan exchanged some words with Cowboys fans sitting close to the field.

Stadium. Maybe the Cowboys' offense really is as explosive as it looked. Maybe Terrell Owens will stay on his present pace of 32 touchdowns. Maybe Romo really is the second coming of Roger Staubach.

Maybe they're really that good.

Or maybe the Giants' defense, which always has been the team's engine and its fuel whenever they've been good, is really that bad. Maybe they are as soft as they looked last night, and as slow, and as incapable of tackling, and as hapless against the run. Maybe Owens is simply that much better than everyone else in the NFL, and so he'll always manage to be 10 yards open whenever a ball is heading his way.

Of course, that doesn't explain why Jason Witten suddenly looked like a combination of Mike Ditka, John Mackey, and Antonio Gates last night. Somehow, series after series, drive after drive, the Cowboys' perfectly serviceable tight end was left alone to do as he pleased, however he pleased, whenever he pleased on the way to 116 yards.

Michael Strahan was a nonfactor, but unless getting Strahan back for the first game meant that the Giants could get Lawrence Taylor, Harry Carson, and Sam Huff back, too, it honestly wouldn't have made a bit of difference. From the start, it seemed like the Cowboys were playing with the fast-forward button, playing at a different speed.

And the Giants were stuck on pause.

Fret over Manning's shoulder all you want over the next few days, but doctors, rest, and ibuprofen can help ease that. Fixing the Giants' defense? That's a little more complicated. And a lot more complex. ■

Eli, Osi, Jacobs Injured In Loss To Cowboys By Paul Schwartz

At the finish, Eli Manning was on the sideline, his right shoulder bruised and tight, his evening over and done after a sterling performance in the season opener was washed over by an overflow of rotten defense.

Manning, running back Brandon Jacobs, and defensive end Osi Umenyiora were all injury casualties last night as the Giants engaged in a shootout and ultimately fell victim to their own defenselessness in a 45-35 loss to the Cowboys at hooting and hollering Texas Stadium.

All of a sudden, this new season is at a crisis point for the Giants, not because they are 0-1 but because three key players are hurting. Jacobs in the second quarter of his first career start went down with a sprained medial collateral ligament that figures to keep him out at least a few weeks. Umenyiora didn't make it out of the first defensive series and though X-rays taken of his knee came back negative, there's concern about his status.

Manning (28 of 41, 312 yards) played one of the best games, matching a career high with four touchdown passes, three to Plaxico Burress. But with 7:20 remaining and the Giants trailing 38-28, he was thrown to the turf by rookie linebacker Anthony Spencer on a failed two-point conversion pass. Manning bruised his throwing shoulder on the play but returned to the field after Gibril Wilson intercepted Tony Romo, giving the ball back to the Giants. Manning threw a 9-yard scoring pass to Burress to close the deficit to 38-35 and would have come back in the game again if his defense could have come up with a stop.

It could not, as Romo fired a 51-yard scoring strike to Sam Hurd, who beat a badly trailing R.W. McQuarters to put the game out of reach.

"It got a little tight as time went on," Manning said of his ailing shoulder. "It got a little more sore. If we had gotten the ball back I would have gone in and tried to win the game. When they got that final touchdown and I talked to the coaches. I didn't want to hurt it worse."

Jared Lorenzen finished up for Manning, who will undergo an MRI exam today to uncover the extent of the injury. "I think it's just soreness and we'll be able to get it worked out," he said.

"He played very, very well," Tom Coughlin said of Manning. "It's just a shame we didn't get the win out of it."

The fingerprints of this loss were left by a Giants defense that was even more shabby than last year, despite the presence of a new defensive coordinator, Steve Spagnuolo, and a supposedly more aggressive scheme. Romo looked like Roger Staubach, compiling 345 passing yards and four touchdown passes, two to Terrell Owens. Tight end Jason Witten (6-116, one TD) ran free all night, often easing past a confused-looking Mathias Kiwanuka in his first game at linebacker.

"We couldn't stop them," Coughlin said. "We didn't get the pressure on the quarterback we thought we would get and the coverage aspect of it is kind of baffling."

Michael Strahan did not start after his 36-day holdout, but played quite a bit after Umenyior was forced out.

"It's very easy to say it's a new defense but we're not going to make any excuses," Strahan said. "We got beat, that's the bottom line."

The Giants amassed 22 first downs and 438 total yards but could not get the Cowboys off the field. The Giants trailed 17-16 at halftime, fell behind 38-22 and then staged a comeback that fell short because their defense could not come close to containing Romo.

"We feel like we let the whole offense down," safety Gibril Wilson said. "They scored 35 points and that should be enough."

Derrick Ward replaced Jacobs and rushed for 89 yards and caught a touchdown pass. ■

Regular Season • September 16, 2007
Giants 13 • Packers 35

Woeful Giants

Favre, Green Bay Pick Apart Coughlin's Corps By Paul Schwartz

Eli Manning was back yesterday, ignoring his bruised right shoulder, not only playing, but playing well, making the throws he needed to make, supposedly injecting some inspiration into the Giants in their home opener.

It was a nice medical comeback for Manning, but it accounted for absolutely nothing in terms of tangible results. That's what happens when you put an incompetent defense on the field that stops no one and makes it impossible to have faith that the season can be anything more than 15 more weeks of drudgery.

For the second consecutive game, the Giants performed on defense as if tackling were an option, mounting a pass rush were against their religious beliefs, and covering opposing receivers had secretly been banned. Packers quarterback Brett Favre's uniform didn't need to be run through the washing machine; he was barely touched as he carved up an inept defense, setting the stage for the Giants' 35-13 loss to Green Bay that immediately set this season on precarious footing.

The Giants are 0-2 for the first time since 1996, which happened to be the final year for lame-duck coach Dan Reeves. With Tom Coughlin granted just a one-year contract extension, this season could assume the feel of that walk-the-plank inevitability unless things change in a hurry.

"I think we are a better football team than we've shown," Coughlin said. "Obviously I don't have any real grounds for saying that, it is just a belief. I do believe we are all in it together and I do believe we are all embarrassed."

Manning (16 of 29, 211 yards, 1 TD, 1 INT) said his right shoulder did not bother him at all. "Physically I feel fine; mentally I am upset about the loss," he said.

He should also be upset with Amani Toomer and Jeremy Shockey for mindless penalties in the red zone, and also incensed with the way his defense refuses to compete. After getting shredded for 45 points last week in Dallas, the Giants have allowed 80 points, the most given up in their first two games since Allie Sherman's crew was blistered for 86 in the first two games of 1966.

Other than a 38-yard touchdown run from some rookie named DeShawn Wynn, the Packers didn't get much going on the ground. But oh, how they passed the ball. Favre (29 of 38, 286 yards, 3 TDs, 1 INT) completed 14 straight passes in the second half, including 11 of 11 in the third quarter as the Giants, trailing 14-13, faded down the stretch as the Packers piled on 21 fourth-quarter points.

This was mostly short, quick stuff that Favre—who passed John Elway to become the NFL's all-time leader in wins for a quarterback with 149—said he was executing "as well as we have in recent memory." He can thank the Giants sieve of a defense for that.

(opposite) Shockey awaits the start of the game.

Manning uncorks a pass during first half action against the Green Bay Packers.

Is there any hope that things can get better as they head to Washington next weekend?

"We don't really have a choice," defensive end Osi Umenyiora said. "We're 0-2 right now, we're not going to get any worse, that I can promise. I'm not sitting over here guaranteeing we're going to win the game but I guarantee we're going to play better."

Things got out of hand in a hurry in the fourth quarter. Favre pump-faked one safety, James Butler, up into the air and then waited until tight end Donald Lee ran past the other safety, Gibril Wilson, for a 3-yard touchdown pass. Rookie Ahmad Bradshaw fumbled away the ensuing kickoff, the Packers took over on the Giants' 22-yard line and soon enough, Favre was hitting Donald Driver for another score.

With the Giants trailing 28-13, the first lusty boos came when on third-and-18 Manning dumped off to Derrick Ward for an eight-yard gain. That triggered a mass exit from the building with a hefty 10:30 left to play. At least those who made a hasty retreat weren't chanting "Fi-re Cough-lin" as they did the last time the Giants played here and were embarrassed by the Saints on Christmas Eve.

"No hope is lost here," said defensive end Michael Strahan, who continues to search for his first sack of the season. "We're professionals, you take your whipping like a man . . . but the one thing you can't do is quit." ∎

'Pack' It In For Big Blue By Steve Serby

The Giants all know the tradition, because it stares them in the face every day. A shrine to Lawrence Taylor, with his gold nameplate (#56, 1981-93) sits between the lockers of Steve Smith and Craig Dahl. Harry Carson's nameplate (#53, 1976-88) rests above Dahl's corner locker by the entrance to the locker room. George Martin's nameplate (#75, 1975-88) is not far to the left of where Michael Strahan dresses.

There is no defense for the New York Giants today. Who would have thought Eli Manning would become the least of the franchise's problems this quickly?

You would think that the sight of the gritty Manning, refusing to let his teammates down by willing himself back on the field, would have inspired Big Blue to get after Brett Favre just a little. Nope. Manning didn't only play with a contused right shoulder yesterday, he played with a contused and confused defense, one that has surrendered 80 points, more than any Big Blue outfit over the first two games of any season since 1966, when Wellington Mara had to listen to his constituency sing "Good-bye All-ie" during a 1-12-1 disaster.

Perhaps NFL Commissioner Roger Goodell can institute a cheating exemption for the 0-2 Giants, humiliated 35-13 losers yesterday to the Packers.

They made Brett Favre (29-for-38, 286 yards, 3 TDs) look young again, as if he were playing in a schoolyard, dinking and dunking off a three-step drop, completing 14 straight passes at one juncture, taking what Big Blue gave him, which was plenty. It was almost as if Paul Hornung were on the sidelines videotaping the signals of already-beleaguered Giants defensive coordinator Steve Spagnuolo.

The Giants (one sack) couldn't rush the passer. "[Favre's] a gunslinger, he's not gonna sit back there and hold that sucker," Strahan said.

Tom Coughlin said: "We blitzed, we tried to pressure with four, we tried to pressure with five, we pressured with six, and we are not getting there."

Take your pick: It's the new attacking system. "I'm not gonna use that as excuse, but you gotta gain confidence in what you're doing," Strahan said. "You can't be guessing out there."

It's the players on the field. "He's putting us in the proper position to make plays, we're just not making the plays . . . that's all our fault," Osi Umenyiora said.

Where do we begin? With Corey Webster's 22-yard pass interference penalty late in the first quarter when Favre was pinned at his 5-yard line? With Webster getting beaten deep for 46 yards by rookie James Jones on the Pack's opening scoring drive? "They tried to bump and James Jones caught

a deep ball on them and then they got out of it," Donald Driver said.

With Strahan dropping in coverage and dropping an interception? With Gibril Wilson beaten by tight end Donald Lee for a 3-yard TD pass early in the fourth quarter? With no one bothering to cover Driver in the back of the end zone moments later?

Perhaps the Giants should have drafted eight cornerbacks. "Obviously, there was some elusiveness we didn't necessarily contend with," Coughlin said.

But now, some reassuring words from Strahan. "I've seen worse," he said. He must be tickled he came back for more of this. "The key thing is don't panic. Did we play the way we wanted to play, or expected to play? Absolutely not. But at the same time, those things are gonna happen to you, it's all about how you handle the aftereffect. When it's happening, trust me, it's killing you."

George Martin, starting at the George Washington Bridge and stopping at Giants yesterday on his way to the Golden Gate Bridge, began a four-month cross-country walk called "A Journey for 9/11," and the shame of it was he didn't take the Giants defense with him.

"As a defense we should be embarrassed; as a team we should be embarrassed," Umenyiora said.

It looks like a long season. ■

Regular Season • September 23, 2007
Giants 24 • Redskins 17

Giant D-Light

Goal-line Stand Caps Comeback, Avoids 0-3 Start By Paul Schwartz

All they had built to get here—the retribution for what had been a downtrodden defense, the personal turnaround for Plaxico Burress, the comeback engineered by Eli Manning, the fight out of a 17-3 hole in a most hostile of surroundings, the raw fear of falling to an 0-3 abyss—it all was about to unravel for the Giants as they frantically searched for their first victory.

A run of 21 unanswered points had shocked a record crowd of 90,803 at FedEx Field, thrusting the Giants into a 24-17 lead. But now things were getting sticky.

Redskin quarterback Jason Campbell was piecing together a drive, and on third-and-13 he found Antwaan Randle El for 20 yards, and suddenly the Skins had first-and-goal on the Giant 1-yard line, with slightly less than a minute remaining and not a single timeout left.

One yard. That was all there was standing in the way of an inspiring victory or a dreaded plummet into the treacherous uncertainty of overtime.

"We came in here basically telling ourselves we need to win or that's probably the end of our season right there," surmised defensive end Justin Tuck.

For a defense that had allowed an NFL-high 80 points in the first two losses, this had the makings of an impossible challenge, even after stopping the Redskins stone-cold in a second half dominated by the Giants.

"Everything we've been taught since day one has to come into play—great tackling and getting off the ball," safety Gibril Wilson said. "Everything has to be perfect down there."

The imperfect defense played a perfect series and, four downs later, after some questionable time management by the Redskins and a final hauldown of a slipping Ladell Betts by Tuck, the Giants were dancing off the field, no longer winless after resuscitating their season with a 24-17 triumph dripping with improbability.

"That's an amazing way to win a game," Manning gushed.

Added Tuck: "To win a game like this, and we needed a fourth-down play on the goal line, you can't write a story better than that."

The story was in real danger of needing a rewrite with the Skins surging for the tie. Campbell on first down, with 51 seconds left, followed some debatable orders from his sideline and spiked the ball, wasting a down to stop the clock. He then looked for Mike Sellers, but the fullback was blanketed by linebacker Kawika Mitchell and the pass fell incomplete.

The Giants knew what was coming next.

"Of course they were going to come to my side," defensive end Osi Umenyiora said. "Where else were they going to go? I was like, well, it's now o never."

(opposite) Plaxico Burress sprints downfield on a 33-yard touchdown reception in the fourth quarter.

AP/Wide World

Derrick Ward searches for yardage against the Washington Redskins.

Running to the right side of the Giant defense—away from Michael Strahan—proved to be the wrong way for the Skins. The 225-pound Betts—and not starter Clinton Portis—was the choice, and on third down Betts was dragged down by Mitchell.

On fourth down, with 25 seconds to go, Betts never got untracked and as he slipped Tuck was there, with rookie Aaron Ross also charging in, to finally allow the Giants to exhale.

"We kept fighting on the road against a very good team, a 2-0 team," Giant coach Tom Coughlin said.

Said Umenyiora: "Especially to stop 'em like that, a goal-line stand, greatest feeling in the world.

The Giants got off th canvas to win this one. The Redskins (2-1) scored 17 straight points to go ahead 17-3 at halftime. Manning fumble off a blind-side hit by Andre Carter—who raced past left tackle David Diehl—led to the

first Redskin TD, and a 49-yard pass to Santana Moss led to the second.

Burress dropped three passes in the first half and, by his own admission, was terrible. But he awakened in the third quarter, as did his offensive teammates.

A 21-yard pass to Jeremy Shockey led to the first of two one-yard scoring bursts by Reuben Droughns as the Giants took the opening kickoff o the second half and closed the deficit to 17-10.

A highlight-reel 33-yard scoring catch-and-run by Burress with 5:32 left gave the Giants their winning points and then they hung on, with one yard to spare.

"I think," Umenyiora said, "this is the beginning of something good." ■

No Points For Skins (Or Critics)

By George Willis

Things had gotten so bad, the criticism so constant, that Giant nose tackle Barry Cofield avoided showing his face in public last week.

"I wasn't going out to dinner," he said. "I was eating at home, eating soup, and I was depressed."

Being part of a defense that had surrendered a league-high 80 points in the first two games of an NFL season will create that kind of shame. Especially when that defense is betraying a heritage of great units that have defined a storied franchise.

"We knew we were better than what we had played," Cofield said, "but when you go out there and give up 40 points a game, you have to start questioning whether we're cursed."

Alas, there is no need for any voodoo or magic potions, and no need for Cofield to bury his 6-foot-4, 306-pound body in his bedroom any longer.

Not after the Giant defense finally arrived for the 2007 season, securing a 24-17 victory over the Redskins yesterday with a game-winning goal-line stand that would hav made Harry Carson and Lawrence Taylor proud.

Finally, the Giant defense showed some moxie, spotting the Redskins a 17-3 lead before posting a second-half shutout that allowed Eli Manning and the Giants offense to score 21 unanswered points and turn a must-win game into a much-needed victory.

The 1-2 Giants still have a season, especially if the defense continues its second- half performance, where it limited the Redskins to 81 net yards and forced four punts and a fumble before securing the game with a goal-line stand on the Redskins' final possession.

If the Giants make the postseason (which is still a big if), they will point to this goal-line stand as the turning point. After watching the Giants rally to tie the game at 17-17 on two touchdown runs by Reuben Droughns and taking the lead 24-17 on a 33-yard catch and run by wide receiver Plaxico Burress, the Redskins tried to answer, moving from the Giant 35 to a first down at the Giant 1 with 58 seconds left.

"The only thing we're thinking is to stop them," said linebacker Antonio Pierce.

On first down, the Redskins spiked the ball to stop the clock. On second down, fullback Mike Sellers dropped a pass in the flat. On third down, running back Ladell Betts tried to bull through the middle of the line but was stopped cold by Kawika Mitchell.

Then it was fourth down with 25 seconds left and counting. Betts tried the left side, where the Redskins had running success earlier in the game. But he ran into a wall of blue led by safety James Butler.

"That feeling I had running off the field after making that stop, I'll never forget it," Cofield said. "To be able to get a stop like that in a division game on the road, it's a great feeling."

No doubt the Redskins helped with some questionable play calling and defensive lapses, but the Giant defense enjoyed its moment of vindication after a week of getting trashed for being among the worst in the NFL over the first two weeks.

"You can't ask for [the defense] to play much better than they did," said Burress. "They stopped those guys on the 12-inch line for three plays. They've taken a lot of [criticism] the last few weeks. I'm just happy those guys can smile a little bit."

There weren't a lot of " told you so's" being tossed around the Giant locker room after the win. It was more relief than anything else.

"We're really fed up with all of the things that have been said about us," said Giant defensive end Osi Umenyiora. "We knew we were better than the way we played." Yesterday they proved it. Finally. ■

Regular Season • September 30, 2007
Giants 16 • Eagles 3

Sacks Maniac

Dozen Tie NFL Mark As Giants Flatten Philly By Paul Schwartz

During the week, members of the Giants defense decided they were all hungry, and the only way to satiate their appetite was to eat up the opposition.

"I was in the training room, I was telling [Justin] Tuck, 'I'm hungry man, I got to eat,' " Osi Umenyiora said.

Consider Umenyiora and the entire Giants defense full, stuffed, and absolutely gorged.

A unit that in the first two weeks of the season was ravaged on the field and savaged by critics off it has suddenly become a fearsome bunch.

Last night, behind a ferocious performance from Umenyiora, the Giants tied an NFL record with 12 sacks of poor, pummeled Donovan McNabb. Umenyiora broke the franchise record with six sacks, and the result was a suffocating 16-3 victory over the rival Eagles in front of an appreciative full house at Giants Stadium.

"Unbelievable . . . I've never seen anything like it," receiver Amani Toomer said. At 2-2, after an 0-2 start, the Giants have plowed back and along the way dropped the Eagles to 1-3. Incredibly, the Eagles last week exploded for 56 points against the Lions, with McNabb enjoying the finest passing day of his career.

One week later, he was flat on his back most of the evening, as a second-year left tackle named Winston Justice was completely unable to deal with the fury that was Umenyiora.

"I never had a game like that before, man," Umenyiora said after breaking the team record of 4.5 sacks in a game by Pepper Johnson and falling one short of the NFL single-game sack record of seven, set by former Chiefs linebacker Derrick Thomas.

"This guy honestly dominated the game," linebacker Antonio Pierce said. "You heard about Lawrence Taylor and I don't want to say it was a Lawrence Taylor-type performance, but this guy dominated the game. If he didn't get the sack he caused some body else to get the sack."

Many Giants players were stunned the Eagles did not eventually find a way to help Justice—starting in place of injured William Thomas—with double-team blocks with a tight end or chips from a running back. It wasn't as if Umenyiora sneaked up on anyone, as four of his sacks came in the first half.

"Was I surprised? Actually I was flabbergasted," Umenyiora said. "After the first couple they should have done something about that. He's a talented young kid. It was just one of those nights."

Joining in the sack race were Mathias Kiwanuka with three, Justin Tuck with two and Michael Strahan with one, which came with 7:25 left in the second quarter when he dropped McNabb for a three-yard loss.

It was career sack No. 133.5 for Strahan, who came into the game tied with Lawrence Taylor for the franchise lead. Taylor was on the sidelines watching the defensive carnage.

(opposite) Ward leaps for extra yards as Amani Toomer looks on.

Burress holds on for a key touchdown reception against the Eagles.

"Osi won't break my record," Strahan said, jokingly, "but he did great."

This was quite a way for first-year defensive coordinator Steve Spagnuolo to debut against the team he spent eight years with as an assistant coach. The overwhelming defensive display was needed, as the Giants were ineffective on offense and unable to take advantage of an uncharacteristically sloppy (15 penalties for 132 yards) showing from the Eagles.

The Giants led 7-0 at halftime after Plaxico Burress leaped between defensive backs Sheldon Brown and Quintin Mikell for a nine-yard touchdown. In the third quarter, leading 10-0, the Giants finally gained more breathing room and fittingly, their defense provided the points.

This time, pressure wasn't what nailed McNabb. He simply lost the ball while fading back, for an aborted play. Linebacker Kawika Mitchell beat running back Correll Buckhalter to the ball and lumbered 17 yards for the touchdown to make it 16-0 (the extra point was missed) with 1:30 left in the third quarter.

Eli Manning was not sharp. Looking to extend the lead after dominating throughout the first half, Manning from the Eagles 15 with 1:17 left before halftime fired to Jeremy Shockey but linebacker Omar Gaither sniffed out the play and darted directly in front of Shockey for the interception.

The Eagles were severely depleted, playing without five starters, including their most dangerous weapon, running back Brian Westbrook. The Giants got healthy with a devastating defensive display.

"We are now 2-2; we give ourselves a chance to be in the hunt," coach Tom Coughlin said. ■

Donovan McNabbed By Steve Serby

The Giants did not come to praise Donovan McNabb, they came to bury him, and at the end of the night, McNabb wasn't just the controversial black quarterback of the Eagles, he was their black-and-blue quarterback.

On a night when Michael Strahan became the Giants' career sack leader (133.5) with Lawrence Taylor in the house, Chief Osi Umenyiora (club-record six sacks) was the one who looked most like LT coming around the corner on a night all the men in blue played like a bunch of crazed dogs.

It must have looked like a Big Blue wave to McNabb, Antonio Pierce blitzing up the middle and Umenyiora, Strahan, Justin Tuck (two sacks), and Mathias Kiwanuka (three sacks) flying around the edges at him. The Giants, ferocious 16-3 winners, sacked No. 5 five times in the first half, and an NFL-record-tying 12 in all.

In the trainer's room before the game, Umenyiora said to Tuck: "Man, I'm hungry. I need to eat!"

Then he turned into Henry VIII.

And in the midst of their buffet on their sidelines, the Blew By You crunch bunch punctuated their feeding frenzy by pretending to feed themselves.

"When somebody gets one, you want one," Strahan said. "When somebody gets two, you want more."

Never mind that a better team would have blown the Eagles out.

Never mind that Umenyiora, the Nigerian Nightmare, went through a second-year turnstile named Winston Justice, who was playing because starting left tackle William Thomas was not. Umenyiora even missed a sure sack that would have given the Giants the record alone and tied him with Derrick Thomas for the single-game record.

"(Umenyiora) really does a great job coming off the corner," Hall of Fame Harry Carson said.

Never mind that McNabb had to hand the ball off to Correll Buckhalter because Brian Westbrook, the Liberty Bell's Tiki Barber, was a spectator.

Never mind that Eli Manning will need to avoid the big mistake, especially in the red zone, and get his team in the end zone more than once.

Never mind that he better start throwing the ball to Jeremy Shockey.

It often isn't whom you play, it's when you play them, and this was the absolute perfect time to play the Eagles.

After two weeks in which Big Blah surrendered 80 points and had the worst defense in the league, coordinator Steve Spagnuolo has morphed into Bill Belichick. If you didn't know any better, you would have thought he had been mentored by Eagles defensive guru Jim Johnson. "We'd run through a brick wall for that guy," Umenyiora said of Spagnuolo.

Which is precisely what they did.

It means the 2-2 Giants are not quite ready to concede the NFC East to the 4-0 Cowboys. "This," Strahan said, "is a big win for our confidence." Why the Big Blue turnaround? "In a lot of ways, a lot of people don't expect a lot out of us," Strahan said. "Everybody said, 'You're done, you're finished.' "

It was Umenyiora who had guaranteed that McNabb would not put up 56 points on the Giants. It was a good thing he and his friends walked the walk, because the momentum of the night had turned just as Manning, 15 yards from paydirt, was driving with a chance to give the Giants a 14-0 lead in the first half before throwing a grievous red-zone interception to Omar Gaither.

Umenyiora, who had been starving for his first sack entering the game, was asked if he was surprised that there was no help, and therefore no justice, for Justice. "I was flabbergasted," he said. "I think maybe they should have done something about that."

Strahan feared for Justice's safety. "In Philadelphia," Strahan said, "if he goes out and orders some food, they might do something to [him]!"

McNabb threw a late TD pass to Reggie Brown that didn't count because he had crossed the line of scrimmage. On fourth down, Umenyiora, one last time, put McNabb down—and out.

"I've never had a game like that before," Umenyiora said with a smile. And he likely won't have one like that anytime soon. ■

Regular Season • October 7, 2007
Giants 35 • Jets 24

Giant Beat Down

Big Blue's 28-point, 2nd-half Outburst Sinks Jets By Paul Schwartz

The evidence was mounting yesterday that the Giants were going to do everything in their power to lose the Battle of New York.

Eli Manning's quarterback rating at halftime was 0.0. Plaxico Burress did not have a single catch. Brandon Jacobs had given away seven points via a fumble. And rookie cornerback Aaron Ross was banished to the bench, having violated team rules earlier in the weekend, not once stepping on the field by decree of Tom Coughlin. At halftime, after the Jets had rung up 10 points in the last 33 seconds, Giants trotted off to the sound of jeers, trailing 17-7 in front of their own season-ticket holders in a building both teams call home.

"Sometimes you're got to win some of these ugly ones and step up to have a great second half," Manning said. Forget about a step-up. This was a leap.

Showing a resiliency that is fast-becoming a trademark, the Giants roared back. Manning couldn't miss. Jacobs wouldn' go down, Burress stiff-armed his way into the end zone, and Ross, finally unleashed, made a pair of game-changing plays. His first career interception halted a Jets drive in the shadow of the Giants end zone and his second career interception of a soft Pennington toss sealed the deal with a 43-yard touchdown return, icing the surging Giants wild 35-24 victory over the reeling Jets.

"Really," linebacker Antoni Pierce said, "the two biggest plays of the game were by Aaron Ross."

The third straight win for the Giants (3-2) featured retribution at every turn, as they scored the final 21 points of the game to send the Jets (1-4) deeper into non-contention well before Halloween.

"Believe me, it makes you sick to your stomach," said Pennington, who was intercepted three times. The Giants were sickened themselves by a miserable offensive first-half showing. They basically handed the Jets 10 points and in Manning's estimation "played as poorly as we could." Rather than panic facing a 10-point deficit, the Giants went to their ground game and Jacobs (20-100, 1 TD) began ripping off yards and scored on a 19-yard rumble on the opening possession of the third quarter. The Giants had to absorb another blow when Leon Washington took the ensuing kickoff 98 yards to make it 24-14. From there, it was all Giants. Manning (10 of 15, 164 yards, 2 TDs in the second half) found Jeremy Shockey slanting for 13 yards for his first TD catch of the season. Early in the fourth quarter, Pennington tried a lob to a double-covered Jerricho Cotchery and Ross leaped to pick the ball off at the Giants two-yard line.

That's when Burress really went to work. He did all his damage (5-124) after halftime and saved his worst abuse for cornerback Andre Dyson. Faced with an all-out blitz, Manning got the ball out quickly, finding Burress on the left sideline for what should have been

(opposite) Sam Madison tries to defend, but Lauvernues Coles held on for the reception.

Eli Manning tries to escape a sack against the Jets.

a six-yard gain. Burress, though, planted an outrageous stiff-arm on Dyson, dispatching the defender as if he were a rag doll and then tiptoed the sideline before sprinting past a final, futile Dyson dive for a 53-yard TD and a 28-24 Giants lead with 7:52 left. "I know if I can get my palm on the crown of their helmet they won't be able to get their hands on me," said Burress, who continues to play despite a sprained right ankle. "I have to get him down any way I can," Dyson said glumly. "He made a great play." Ross ended any Jets comeback ideas when he jumped a route run by Cotchery and with 3:15 remaining put Pennington out of his misery with his interception return for a touchdown. It was quite a personal turn-

around for Ross, who was punished by Coughlin for what likely was either arriving late or missing a team meeting on Saturday.

"It was a mistake," Ross said. "I feel like I responded really well." After the 12-sack eruption last week against the Eagles, the Giants notched one in this game and it didn't come until Osi Umenyiora finally got to Pennington with 2:55 to go. Still, it was a solid performance by the defense, completely shutting down the Jets rushing attack (25-55).

"We feel like the Giants should always be on top here," Michael Strahan said. Thanks to a dominating second half, they are for now. ∎

Rookie Responds By Steve Serby

Maybe this is the game that ultimately saves Tom Coughlin, and buries the 1-4 Jets. The game when everyone remembers how the old-school head coach, true to principles forever loved by Wellington Mara, even as the lame-duck coach of the Giants, calls the No. 1 draft choice from Texas to his office yesterday morning and tells him he won't be playing for the first half of the Battle of New York because he violated a team rule.

And maybe cornerback Aaron Ross will be remembered as the kid who saved Coughlin.

There were all kinds of reasons for Giants 35, Jets 24. On the Giant side, Eli Manning bringing his team back in the second half and Plaxico Burress stiff-arming Andre Dyson all the way back to Weeb Ewbank Hall on a 53-yard TD romp down the sidelines that gave the Giants the lead midway through the fourth quarter. On the Jets side, it was another fourth-quarter nightmare from Chad Pennington (2 of his 3 INTs), that will inevitably prompt premature howls for Kellen Clemens. The New York Frick and Frac Exchange pass rush on Manning, and an offense that has no chance if Thomas Jones cannot run effectively (13-36) since the quarterback can't scare anyone deep.

But first and foremost, thank Aaron. "Down the road," Coughlin said,

"that will be the best thing that will happen for Aaron.

Down the road, Ross' two fourth-quarter interceptions might prove to be the best thing that will happen for Coughlin, whose 3-2 Giants have no reason not to be 6-2 at the break after games against the Falcons, 49ers and Dolphins.

He returned the second one 43 yards for a touchdown at a time when Pennington, from his 39, was threatening to move against a Munch Bunch that had yet to feast on him and finished with one sack, or 11 fewer than a week ago, and crown themselves kings of the city.

The clock read 3:28 when Pennington, second-and-5, looked for Jerricho Cotchery short to his right.

Game over.

"Once I saw that [bunch] formation and the receiver run that out route, I was able to break on it," Ross said.

Ross thought back on an interception for a touchdown last season against Kansas and said, smiling. "I hadn't had the ball in my hands in almost a year now, so it felt real good," he said.

It felt so good he slowed down and leapt/pranced over the goalline while holding the ball aloft. "That was my Superman," Ross said. Huh? "That's a song I like listening to," he said, and chuckled.

Coughlin was waiting for him on the sideline.

"Great job," Coughlin said.

"Thank you, coach," Ross said. Then he added: "We hugged each other, and that was it."

Ross' first NFL pick came on a grievous Pennington underthrow from the Giant 23 for Cotchery at the 2 early in the fourth quarter when the Jets were trying to take a 31-21 lead. Ross left Coles to help SamMadison.

"It was like a picture-perfect play," Ross said.

When he called him on the carpet, Coughlin did not tell Ross exactly how long he would sit behind Corey Webster. Ross fell silent.

"I knew I had to just stay ready to play; I have to man up to my mistake," he said.

His teammates encouraged him.

"We were all tapping him on the back, telling him, 'Make sure you don't get down on yourself,'" Antonio Pierce said.

Neither Coughlin nor Ross would speak to his indiscretion.

"It'll never happen again," Ross said. "Lesson learned."

Lesson taught. "You have to let the coach handle it the way he wants to handle it," John Mara said. "[GM] Jerry Reese called me this morning to let me know what was going on, and I said, 'Well we gotta support the coach,' and that's the way he chose to handle it. If he had chosen to bench him for the game, that would have been his prerogative." Then Mara let out a big laugh and said: "I'm glad he didn't bench him for th game! ■

Regular Season • October 15, 2007
Giants 31 • Atlanta 10

Flyin' Over

Big Blue At 4-2 After Easy Victory By Paul Schwartz

The goal was simple: Get out to a fast start, something that, at least offensively, the Giants found exceedingly difficult even during their winning streak.

"We wanted to set the tone of the game," Amani Toomer said, "and I think this is the first time we actually did that."

Coming out firing, the Giants entrusted Eli Manning with the keys to the attack last night, giving him the freedom to play pitchand- catch with his receivers inside the fast track of the Georgia Dome. There were stretches, especially early, when Manning was in rhythm and virtually unstoppable as the Giants threatened to blow out the Falcons. It is a measure of how far the Giants have come (and how low the Falcons have sunk) that they were at their best some of the time but not all of the time, but still came away with a solid 31-10 victory to continue their dramatic resurgence.

"It's good to win, no doubt about it," coach Tom Coughlin said, "and we've kind of done it in different ways." This time, there was no need for a second-half comeback, as Manning tossed a touchdown pass to Amani Toomer and used pinpoint passing to set up Reuben Droughns' 1-yard scoring run before the first quarter was complete. That enabled the Giants to get out of the first quarter with a 14-10 lead and set the stage for what followed.

"We knew we had to start fast and maybe take away a little bit out of their bite," guard Chris Snee said. "Kind of take the wind out of 'em a little bit." Rolling along with a four-game winning streak, the Giants (4-2) have long-since put their 0-2 start in the rearview mirror and moved into second place in the NFC East, ahead of the Redskins (3-2) and one game behind the Cowboys (5-1).

During a torrid first-half stretch, Manning (27 of 39, 303 yards, two touchdowns, two interceptions) completed 12 consecutive passes, a run that ended because of a drop by rookie tight end Michael Matthews. Manning also continued his uncanny chemistry with Plaxico Burress (6-97), the receiver who never practices because of a sprained right ankle but still manages to dominate in the games. Burress, in the second quarter, ran under what turned into a 43-yard touchdown pass; he completely dispatched an attempted jam at the line by cornerback Chris Houston and then blew by safety Lawyer Milloy to provid Manning with an open target far downfield. It was Burress' eighth TD catch of the season and made it 21-10.

"I've always said we need him out there at practice, but now I kind of think maybe we don't," Manning said, smiling.

On defense, the Giants overcame an early lapse that resulted in a 67-yard scoring jaunt by Jerious Norwood.

Manning fires a pass in the win over the hapless Falcons.

AP/Wide World

Brandon Jacobs is upended by Falcons linebacker Keith Brooking

Twice, the Giants turned the ball over in their own territory—one on a Manning fumble, the other on an interception—and twice the defense rose up and held the struggling Falcons without a point. The Giants, who have allowed two touchdowns in their last 14 quarters, limited Atlanta to 284 total yards, mainly because they harassed Joey Harrington, sacking him four times.

"I think we're playing so good because we've still got that 0-2 mentality," linebacker Antonio Pierce said. The Falcons needed to use so much manpower to ensure that novice NFL tackles Renardo Foster and Tyson Clabo were not overwhelmed by defensive ends Osi Umenyiora and Michael Strahan that the interior of the offensive line was compromised. That led to sacks up the middle from

Justin Tuck, Pierce, and Fred Robbins. Toomer, early in the fourth quarter, caught the 587th pass of his Giants career, moving him past Tiki Barber and making him the franchise's career leader in receptions.

By then, the Giants were on their way, as they relied in the second half on a bludgeoning running game. Brandon Jacobs (13-86) and Derrick Ward (9-yard TD run) and Droughns (14-90) helped the Giants amass 188 rushing yards.

"Your seeing our big running backs wearing down the defense," center Shaun O'Hara said. "Those are three physical guys." ■

Eli Is Mann Of The Hour By Steve Serby

Ultimately, it won't be Tom Coughlin turning into a player's coach that will save his job.

It will be Eli Manning playing the way a franchise quarterback is supposed to play.

Coughlin convinced ownership during their postseason summit that he was the right man to get Manning to take the next step, and look at the Giants now—4-2, winners of four in a row, one game behind the Cowboys, on a fast track to 6-2 at the bye.

Notice was served last night that the Giants, 31-10 winners over the Falcons, do not always have to beat you with their Munch Bunch pass rush (four more sacks) feasting on quarterbacks.

The Giants do not always have to beat you with Thunder & Enlightening, their Baby Bull tandem of Brandon Jacobs and Derrick Ward . . . and don't forget Reuben Droughns.

They can beat you now with Eli Manning, too.

For 20 minutes last night, 20 minutes that decided the game, they weren't the G-Men as much as they were the E-Men.

When Manning throws the ball like this, when he show this kind of poise and mobility and field vision and command and ring generalship, he can be Marcel Marceau, for all New York will care.

Manning, who had 11 straight completions as one of his goals, completed 12 straight before backup tight end Michael Matthews dropped a gimme during a first half in which Eli looked more like Peyton's big brother, except when he telegraphed an interception over the middle for Plaxico Burress in the final minute.

Manning, stepping into his throws and effortlessly spraying the ball around the Georgia Dome, engineered a pair of touchdown drives in the first quarter and got everyone involved, especially Giants career reception leader Amani Toomer, who didn't catch a pass against the Jets. Manning, off play-action, fired a 5-yard TD pass to Toomer for the first Giants score and set up the second with a 17-yarder to Toomer, masterfully keeping both feet in bounds at the 1. And if it wasn't Toomer, it was Jerem Shockey, too often an afterthought in the beginning of games when he can be the Energizer Bunny.

"We're spreading the ball all around, and that's when we're at our best, we can mix things up and get everybody involved," Manning said.

And if it wasn't Toomer and Shockey, it was, of course, Burress, Eli's Marvin Harrison, streaking down the middle past safety Lawyer Milloy, frozen by play-action, to catch a perfect 43-yard TD bomb from Manning t give the Giants a 21-10 halftime lead. Not bad for a guy with a sprained ankle. "I've always said I think we need him out there to practice," Manning joked, "and now, I'm starting to maybe say we don't."

By intermission, Manning had passed for 208 yards, on his way to 303 on 27-of-39 passing

"He had the hot hand, no doubt about it," Coughlin said.

Even with the threat of Tiki Barber behind him, there were disturbing signs that Manning might be regressing. Giants fans began cursing the football gods, asking how Ernie Accorsi, the GM at the 2004 NF Draft, could possibly have preferred Manning to Ben Roethlisberger and Philip Rivers.

Last year, outside the Colts' euphoric Super Bowl locker room, Manning's mother, Olivia, exulted that now that Peyton had finally gotten the monkey off his back, next it would be Eli's turn, and, ahem, this was certainly not the time to dismiss it out of hand as wishful thinking.

A stone-faced Eli waved off reporters that night and showed up in Albany this summer with a new resolve and a new quarterbacks coach (Chris Palmer)—and even a new body language.

Then, standing up for himself, he fired back at Barber for questioning his leadership abilities.

Then, fulfilling the obligation of the franchise quarterback, he showed a toughness tha belies his goody two-shoes appearance and fought off a right shoulder sprain to be there on game day for his team and teammates. Then came a wondrous 20 minutes last night. Half-Manning, half-amazing. ∎

Regular Season • October 21, 2007
Giants 33 • 49ers 15

Giants Can

Big Blue Blats 49ers For Fifth Straight Win By Paul Schwartz

It's official. Jeremy Shockey wants to change sides. "I wish I could switch over and play a little defensive end for this defense," Shockey said yesterday in the aftermath of yet another Giants victory. "It's definitely a great feeling seeing those guys have fun with it. I would like to go down and try to get in on it, for sure."

Why not? Put Shockey on the edge and let him go get the quarterback and, given what's transpired the past month, he'll likely be shaking to a new sack dance before long.

One more game, one more deadly dose of dominating, harassing, punishin defense doled out by a unit that has sparked a remarkable turnaround and taken the entire team along for the ride. A unit that scored on its own– with Osi Umenyiora's clinic-like sack/forced fumble/recovery/touchdown return–caused four total turnovers that led to 24 points, making it easy pickings in a 33-15 thumping of the sagging 49ers at sun-drenched Giants Stadium.

Back-to-back routs of bad teams the past two weeks lifts the Giants to 5-2 for the fourth consecutive year under Tom Coughlin and increases the winning streak to five games, suddenly allowing the Giants to think big thoughts as they scan the NFC and see what's out there.

"Putting teams away that we should put away is the sign of a good team," said Amani Toomer, whose first-quarter touchdown catch gave him a franchis scoring record.

The torrid Giants now pack up for a most unusual road trip, as later this week they head to London to face the winless Dolphins (0-7) Sunday at Wembley Stadium. It will be the NFL's first ever regular-season game in Europe and will feature a white-hot team against a miserable one.

"That's scary," said linebacker Antonio Pierce, whose interception of abused San Francisco quarterback Trent Dilfer set up the final Giants touchdown, Eli Manning's 2-yard fastball to Shockey. "Of course we're going to be crowned as the gods and the kings and they're going to be crowned as just a losing team. I don't look at it that way. Every team comes away with a win eventually and we're just going to hope we're not the team to give them their first victory."

That mentality is what may separate this team from the previous early-season demons that often flopped once winter set in. "I like this team in terms of their approach," Coughlin said.

Other than a few bothersome lapses in the kicking operation, the Giants coasted. They sacked Dilfer six times, with Michael Strahan (2.5) getting his first multiple-sack game of the season. They gift-wrapped 17 points for the offense by setting Manning up on the San Francisco 27, 30 and five yard lines. "I felt like we were

(opposite) Manning, flushed out of the pocket, looks downfield for a receiver.

Michael Strahan celebrates his first quarter sack against the 49ers.

getting the ball on their side of the 50-yard line all day long," center Shaun O'Hara said. "Our defense has really been our heart and soul."

Trailing 7-6, the Giants got the ball back when Dilfer in the second quarter lost the handle on an exchange and Umenyiora recovered on the 49ers 27. Four plays later, Brandon Jacobs (18 carries, career-high 107 yards) bulled in to make it 13-7. On the very next play, cornerback Sam Madison jumped in front of Arnaz Battle for an interception, leading to a Lawrence Tynes field goal.

In the third quarter, Umenyiora obliterated any shot left tackle Jonas Jennings had of blocking him and laid blind-side hit on Dilfer, causing a fumble that he picked up in stride and raced 75 yards untouched for his second career touchdown.

"He made it look simple, but it is not," Coughlin said.

"It was perfect ... textbook," marveled Pierce. "It will definitely be on somebody's coaching tape."

The dominance allowed the Giants to shut down their offense in the second half, although they wanted to produce more than 49 total yards and four first downs.

"We didn't have the ball much and had a strong lead," Manning said. That is a good problem to have.

The Giants haven't lost since Pierce blew an air horn in the locker room and he says it's no coincidence.

"It was just setting the tone for something else, for the bigger picture," he said. "I can't be credited for it, I just sparked something. We call it the revolution. We were 0-2, we needed a needed movement." The movement is 5-0 and off to London. ■

Osi Enjoys An LT-like Afternoon

By Bart Hubbuch

AP/Wide World

Shades of LT. Giants defensive end Osi Umenyiora wanted no part of the Lawrence Taylor comparisons afterward, but he sure looked like the second coming of No. 56 yesterday on a spectacular, game clinching play against the San Francisco 49ers.

Umenyiora's coaches and teammates almost didn't know which part of his third-quarter highlight reel moment to marvel at most: the sack, the forced fumble, the mid-air fumble recovery or the 75-yard touchdown return.

All of the above, linebacker Antonio Pierce decided.

"That's a lot of production on one play right there," Pierce said after the Giants' 33-15 win. "That's going to look good on the stat sheet. That's a good demonstration of what kind of talent he has."

The Giants battered backup 49ers quarterback Trent Dilfer with six-sack feeding frenzy, but it was Umenyiora's display less than two minutes into the second half that left the crowd and the locker room buzzing long afterward.

San Francisco was on the march at the Giants' 15-yard line and about to cut into a 19-7 deficit when Umenyiora swooped in from the right side, slammed Dilfer to the ground while batting the ball out of his hand, then somehow caught it,

got to his feet and sprinted the other way to the end zone.

Game over.

"It was just a tremendous effort by me," Umenyiora said, laughing "Seriously, I was just in the right place in the right time. It was a lucky play, man." Once he caught the ball, Umenyiora's biggest worry was getting caught from behind. It would have been an ugly locker room for the fifth- year pro this week if that had happened.

"I couldn't get caught simply because I've talked so much trash about how fast I am," Umenyior said. "They couldn't catch me, because I'd

never have heard the end of it."

The sack allowed Umenyiora to take the team lead with eight sacks, and it should boost his pocketbook this week, too. That's because Michael Strahan started a high-stakes weekly pot for the defensiv line yesterday, with the winner determined by that game's production.

"We'll see how I did (today)," Umenyiora joked. But Umenyiora's face turned serious when the Taylor comparison was brought up.

"I'm not even going touch that one," he said. "That's the greatest player in Giants history. I'm just going to savor my moment." ■

Regular Season • October 28, 2007
Giants 13 • Dolphins 10

Giants Pass

Big Blue Cap Brutal Trip With Ugly Win By Paul Schwartz

The end of a grueling and historic four days could not come soon enough for the Giants, who were grinding to the finish of a wet and muddy contest that was deteriorating at an alarming rate. All of a sudden, the first NFL regular-season game ever played outside of North America was threatening to devolve into the worst loss ever for the Giants on foreign soil. An untidy but effective 13-0 lead bent and wobbled but didn't break, and after escaping last night with a 13-10 victory over the still-winless Dolphins at Wembley Stadium, the Giants were eager to get dry, get fed, and then get home.

"The biggest priority is eat something, enjoy the win," center Shaun O'Hara said, looking forward to one final night here. "Maybe grab a pint. Or 10." The ale would certainly have had a bitter aftertaste had the Giants (6-2) not increased their winning streak to six and achieved what they knew they must in this first International Series event. A crowd of 81,176, mostly cheering for the "home team" Dolphins but often cheering and whistling at most any action, witnessed a game that might have the Brits saying "No thanks" the next time the American version of football is offered.

A steady rain turned the thin grass soccer field into a quagmire and obliterated the passing game the Giants wanted to use to exploit Miami's man-to-man defensive coverage. Eli Manning threw for an anemic 59 yards,

completing eight of his 22 passes. You knew something was terribly wrong when Manning was more effective with his legs (career-high 25 rushing yards, including 10 yards for the Giants only touchdown) than he was with his arm. "With the conditions, we weren't throwing it especially well," Manning said.

The Giants didn't score a point after halftime and had to sweat out a few anxious moments when Cleo Lemon, with 1:54 remaining, hit rookie Ted Ginn Jr. to trim the Giants' lead to three points. When Jay Feely—the former Giants kicker—sent the onside kick rolling out of bounds, all that was left were three kneel-downs by Manning, prompting a loud chorus of boos. "I thought the fans were great and they were loud," Tom Coughlin said, "and the only thing they didn't understand is us kneeling on the ball at the end. I guess you have to know football to understand that."

That about sums up a strange evening that never quite was in synch. A streaker, masquerading as an NFL official undressed, danced, and gyrated wearing nothing but a thong in the shape of a football, delaying the second-half kickof for a few minutes.

"I enjoyed every bit of it," running back Brandon Jacobs said. "That doesn't happen across the water." On

(opposite) Reuben Droughns attempts to slip a tackle on the muddy surface in London.

the Giants' first possession, Manning, from the Miami 3-yard line, overthrew a wide-open Amani Toomer in the back of the end zone, setting a tone that never quit. The British fans were then treated to what was, to be kind, a game devoid of the "cracking" plays the locals were hoping to see. Manning thrust both fists into the air and then knocked on his helmet in disgust after the misfire, forcing the Giants to settle for Lawrence Tynes' 20-yard field goal. Perhaps it was fitting that Tynes' leg produced the first points in this event, as he's the NFL's only Scottish-born player.

The pounding running of Jacobs (23 carries, career-high 131 yards in the slop) set up Manning's rare scoring run. Lemon whiffed on a pass, Michael Strahan pounced on the

Jacobs tries to elude Dolphins' tacklers for extra yards.

ball on the Miami 34-yard line and Tynes nailed his second field goal to make it 13-0. What figured to be an inelegant but routine victory nearly stalled out. The Giants were called for six penalties in the second half, Manning lost the ball on a fumble and Tynes slipped and missed a 29-yard field goal attempt early in the fourth quarter.

Had it not been the dreadful Dolphins (0-8), this might have been a colossal loss of international proportions. "It was definitely a relief," Toomer said. "In the NFL not every game is going to be gorgeous," added O'Hara. "Sometimes you got to go home with the ugly date. It's a lot prettier when you win." On any continent. ■

One Bloody Awful Game By George Willis

If this is the best the NFL has to offer its European fans then they would be wise to stick with their own version of football.

Well, maybe it wasn't that bad at Wembley Stadium yesterday. But certainly the first regular-season NFL game played outside North America wasn't the crowd-thrilling showcase organizers had hoped to see.

The Giants' 13-10 escape over the winles Dolphins was a mess from the muddy, slippery field to the performance of both teams, who ruined themselves with penalties, errant throws, missed field goals, and other costly miscues.

Giants wide receiver Amani Toomer called it "ugly," while running back Brandon Jacobs said, "I don't think people saw the best of us. We left some things out there."

When there's more conversation about a streaker, who sashayed onto the field before the second-half kickoff, than there is about the game itself, you have to wonder whether these international trips are worth the fuss.

"We expected a very difficult ballgame under the circumstances and there's no question we got one," said Giants coach Tom Coughlin.

The grumpy coach who wore a plastic smile all weekend ends his first trip to London with the only souvenir he wanted, a sixth-straight win that improved his team to 6-2 entering a bye week. But the Giants' performance won't make this a restful week.

Rain, wet footballs and slippery turf aren't exclusive to London, and Eli Manning's performance raises questions whether he can be productive in adverse conditions. He wasn't yesterday completing just 8 of 22 passes for 59 yards and failing to generate any points in the second half after a 13-0 lead at halftime.

Penalties, including four during one fourth-quarter drive, nearly wasted a career-high 131 yards rushing by Jacobs. Lawrence Tynes missing a 29- yard field goal the Giants badly needed leading 13-3 with 11:48 to play isn't a good omen either.

"We weren't able to get the kind of points that I thought we might be able to do here," Coughlin said. "We're fortunate and very thankful for the win."

Hopefully, the Europeans hadn't seen enough good American football to know the difference. The sellout crowd spectacled with jerseys from various NFL teams was energized throughout the game despite the on-and-off drizzle. It had the feel of a mini-Super Bowl at times with a pregame show by a Beatles-looking band called "The Feeling." At the opening kickoff, flashbulbs lit up the stadium.

"It's great to be one of the first teams to play a regular-season game here and it was great to get the first win no matter how ugly it was," Toomer said. "This is definitely easier with a win."

The Giants, who had scored at least 30 points in their three previous games didn't want to blame the sloppy turf and wet conditions for their offensive struggles. But they did.

"It was tough at times out there," Manning said. "The wind and rain made playing conditions tough."

Global warming has turned Giants Stadium into a summer villa compared to when Phil Simms had to fight the cold and wind. But that doesn't mean it won't be damp and miserable again when the play the Cowboys there in two weeks.

Manning did score a touchdown on a 10-yard scramble in the second quarter yesterday, but that may have been his only highlight. Most of his passes sailed wide or high.

"We won and that's the important thing," he said.

True. For the third straight season, the Giants are 6-2, but hardly a juggernaut. They leave London knowing they have a week to rest, but much to improve on if they're going to pass the Cowboys.

Playing in the NFL's International Series in front of a foreign audience is someone else's mantle to carry. Let's hope the locals get to see a better game next time. ■

Regular Season • November 11, 2007
Giants 20 • Cowboys 31

Giants Done

Big Blue Comes Up Small vs. 'Boys By Paul Schwartz

Everyone, including the Giants, wanted to know. Just how good are they? Everyone, including the Giants, knew the answer would come last night. After feasting on so many of the dregs of the NFL, the Giants took their six-game winning streak into a firstplace showdown with the rival Cowboys, the division leaders and early favorites to get to the Super Bowl out of the NFC. This would surely provide a litmus test for the surging but largely unproven Giants.

Now they know. At this point, they simply do not measure up. "Absolutely not a better team than us," defensive end Osi Umenyiora said. "They might have played better today, in the second half, but I'll never say they're a better team than us." He doesn't have to say it. The evidence was once again splattered out across the field, just as it was in the season opener. The Giants were able to hang in, battling through a 17-17 first half, but once the Cowboys hit the accelerator the Giants could not locate an extra gear. They were done in by the pinpoint passing of Tony Romo, two touchdown catches by Terrell Owens, not enough firepower from Eli Manning's inconsistent attack, and a rash of debilitating penalties. The result was a resounding 31-20 loss at a raucous and then deflated Giants Stadium.

"The second half was not good enough," Tom Coughlin said. "We were our own worst enemy. We have no excuses. I am disappointed, but I think we have a good football team and we will go back to work now." The chore is to rebound from this slap-down and make sure there are no lasting psychological scars. This setback cost the Giants (6-3) any legitimate shot at the division title. As based on tiebreakers, they are three games behind the Cowboys (8-1). "It is sort of disappointing but it is not the end of the world," Manning said.

Manning came out a distant second in what was billed as a battle of two of the young guns in the NFC. Romo tossed four touchdown passes (he's got eight in two games against the Giants) and completed a crisp 20 of 28. Manning, harassed more than he's been in more than a month, was sacked five times, continually threw underneath to Jeremy Shockey (career-high 12 catches) but could not get much done in the second half (three points) and was called for a ghastly three delay-of-game penalties The Cowboys, losers this season only to the mighty Patriots, took great delight in waylaying the Giants.

"They've been talking all week," claimed receiver Patrick Crayton, who caught a 20-yard touchdown pass in the second quarter. "I think when you are kind of scared of another team like that you kind of have to talk yourself up to really give yourself a chance. It started

(opposite) A dejected Manning after the Giants turned the ball over on downs late in the game.

Brandon Jacobs fights for a 1st down in the 2nd half.

with Brandon Jacobs and it kind of trickled a little bit to some other players."

Jacobs, who rushed for 95 yards, before the first game said the Giants would "Whup their (butt)" but nothing acerbic came out of his mouth this week.

"No, it's not a fair assessment," Jacobs said after hearing Crayton's comments. "I think the Cowboys are a great team and it's not fair for him to come out and say that, because h (stinks), first of all." The Giants faded badly after halftime. The Cowboys took the lead for good on Romo's 25-yard scoring strike to Owens, who badly outran cornerback Sam Madison on a straight fly pattern. "It was all me," Madison said. "One play got away and it hurt this football team."

There was more to come. A holding penalty on rookie tight end Kevin Boss nullified an 83-yard kickoff return by Ahmad Bradshaw to the Dallas two-yard line. Early in the fourth quarter, a holding penalty on right guard Chris Snee called back a Jacobs touchdown run.

A Lawrence Tynes field goal closed the deficit to 24-20 but not for long, as Romo again went to Owens. A mistake in the zone coverage left safety Gibril Wilson too long on Owens, who ran away from Wilson for a 50-yard scoring pass to make it 31-20 with 10:43 left.

If this indeed was a statement game, the Giants did not like what message they sent.

"The statement is we're still a good team," Antonio Pierce said. "We lost. We lost to a good team. That's all that means. Do we want to be 7-2? Of course. We're 6-3 and we're not going to complain about that either." ∎

Romo Rolls, Eli Folds In Giant Mismatch By Steve Serby

On a Star Wars stage where Eli Manning had his chance to make the kind of loud and definite statement Giant fans have been hungering for since he arrived four years ago as their franchise quarterback, it was Tony Romo who delivered the Gettysburg Address.

It was Cowboys 31, Giants 20 because Tony Romo (20-28, 247 yards, 4 TDs) is the fastest gun in the NFC East, too fast for Eli Manning (23-34, 236 yards, 1 TD, 2 INTs) who needed to be Peyton Manning last night to survive this Shootout At The Not-So-OK Corral and convince the skeptics the Giants are something more than a wild-card team that can't beat the Big Boys, especially in the second half of any given season.

If Romo-to-Terrell Owens (6-125 receiving, 2 second-half TDs) is going to dominate Manning-to-Plaxico Burress, then fuggeddaboudit.

When the 6-3 Giants needed him to grab the game by the throat, Manning was sabotaged by a helter-skelter operation lowlighted by three delay-of-game penalties and a critical hold during a touchdown run.

The carefree Romo, meanwhile, looks like he's playing in a schoolyard. Or Wyatt Earp in shoulder pads.

Jerry Jones stopped talking for a second to yell out "Hey Tony!" and walk over to give his always-smiling golden child a hug outside the tunnel.

"I saw where a guy defined beauty as a combination of things that you don't need to add anything to it," Jones said, "and all he needs to do is keep working hard and get it better, but when you look at what he is intangibly and tangibly, you don't need to be adding a lot to that except refine and get better."

The Cowboys were not going to let Brandon Jacobs (23 carries, 95 yards) beat them, and in the second half, they were not going to let Burress (four catches, 24 yards) beat them deep. "They just weren't letting any of us get behind them," Burress said. Jeremy Shockey (12-129, 1 TD), as a result, was Manning's lone lethal weapon

They were going to make Manning find a way to beat them, and he could not, could not go bullet-for-bullet with Romo, who made a mockery of these Folly Red Giants. "We tried to throw some short stuff; they did a good job of tackling our guys," Manning said.

Romo gives you more than a hint of greatness, and Manning still does not. "He's just such an instinctive player; he's got great vision, and he's a great competitor," Cowboys offensive coordinator Jason Garrett said.

With infectious charisma that uplifts teamates. "He's got a lot of [Michael] Irvin in him," Jones said.

Manning is a good quarterback, but the Giants will need him to be great to compete against Romo.

Manning could not overcome Giants crumbling around him—he was sacked five times, while Romo's pocket presence and mobility limited Big Blue to two sacks. "I think most quarterbacks probably today would have been sacked maybe four, five, six times, but he sees the rush and he just escapes and he makes plays," Osi Umenyiora said.

When Owens ran past Gibril Wilson, and Romo delivered him the ball in stride for a 50-yard TD with 10:43 left, it was over.

Eli coming. Not Peyton.

Manning, third-and-10 at the end, was cascaded with boos for throwing a six-yard pass to Reuben Droughns. On fourth-and-4 from the Dallas 31, Manning threw high for Burress

Romo, forever looking for the downfield dagger, had hit Owens in stride past Sam Madison with a 25-yard TD strike that gave the Cowboys a 24-17 lead. Madison was asked what makes Romo so dangerous. "His feet," Madison said.

Manning was asked about Manning vs. Romo. "I'm going against the Dallas defense; that's my only concern," Manning said.

But even he was impressed. "He's playing good football," Manning said.

He was the only quarterback playing super football last night. ∎

Regular Season • November 18, 2007
Giants 16 • Lions 10

Magic In Motown

Mouthy Giants Prevail, Both On And Off Field By Paul Schwartz

When it comes to sorting out the second tier of the NFC, there was nothing bigger than the game yesterday inside Ford Field, which is why the loser felt so very disgusted and the winner so incredibly relieved. And so, when cornerback Sam Madison with 49 seconds remaining tracked a deflection off the hands of receiver Shaun McDonald and snare it in his hands for an interception, an afternoon of defensive dominance and high-wire anxiety ended for the Giants with a 16-10 victory over the Lions, at least one of the combatants could not deal with reality.

"We gave them the football game," declared Lions quarterback Jon Kitna, who threw for 377 yards but was also picked off three times. "In November and December you cannot let a team beat you at your place that is not better than you. This isn't high school football." That claim attracted the attention of Michael Strahan, who got up close and personal with Kitna, sacking him three times in a full day's work that left him weary but still aching for a fight. "Did he really say that?" Strahan asked. "I honestly, in the first half, thought that was probably one of the worst teams we were playing that was 6-3, to be honest with you. So I don't quite understand why Jon would say that. Bottom line is, we're 7-3, they're what, 6-4? Maybe we'll see 'em down the road. If that's the case we'll beat that [butt] again.

"Give him some New York attitude. Come to New York. This may be Motor City, but we'll whip your [butt] still." The intensity after the final whistle reflected the importance of the outcome.

The Giants successfully rebounded from their first-place showdown loss to the Cowboys and moved two games ahead of their nearest challenger (the Lions) in the NFC wild-card race. To do it, the Giants had to knock off a team that had been unbeaten (4-0) and averaging 31 points at home. The Giants also had to withstand the season-ending injury to linebacker Mathias Kiwanuka (broken left fibula) on the second play of the game and a third-quarter hamstring injury that sent Brandon Jacobs to the sideline They also had to overcome a strange offensive showing that had Eli Manning complete 28 of 39 passes for 283 yards, no interceptions but manage just one touchdown drive, forcing three Lawrence Tynes field goals to be enough for a defense that is increasingly carrying too much of a burden. "I think I personally thanked Sam [Madison] for allowing us to get out of there with a win," center Shaun O'Hara said. "At times it felt like trying to draw blood out of a rock." Although they never trailed, the Giants could not build a margin based largely on their ow mistakes. They were driving in the secon quarter

(opposite) Sinorice Moss puts the ball on the turf in the face of opportunistic Lion defenders.

but Sinorice Moss lost the ball on a fumble. They were driving in the third quarter but Jacob was stripped of the ball for a fumble.

When Jeremy Shockey was tackled two yards shy of the end zone, Tynes trotted out and his 20-yard field goal made it a 16-3 Giants lead with 11:15 left With absolutely no running game (2 total rushing yards) to fall back on, Kitna hit four straight passes on a quick-strike 82-yard drive, capped with 4:34 to go when 6-5 rookie Calvin Johnson elevated over 5-8 cornerback Kevin Dockery for a 35-yard touchdown catch. The offense failed miserably to run time off the clock, as Manning was sacked on third down, and the Lions got another shot.

After what looked to be a bogus roughing the passer penalty on Justin Tuck, safety James Butler jumped with

Kevin Jones is hammered in midair by Strahan.

McDonald and came away with his first interception of the season, in the end zone. Again, the offense could not seal the deal, going three-and-out to put the ball back in Kitna's hands with 1:25 remaining. A 27-yard completion to McDonald put the Lions in Giants territory before Madison's interception finally silenced the crowd for good.

"They bailed us out again," guard Chris Snee said. "We should have been able to run that clock out. We didn't do our job." Manning called it "a big step for us."

Tom Coughlin said, simply, "In the NFC, it was a big game." But Strahan was more on point. "To come into Detroit, play a team at 6-3 and win," Strahan said, "trust me, you can't beat that." ■

Big Blue Hero?
The Butler Did It By Steve Serby

The ball, and the ballgame, and quite possibly the wild-card playoffs, and all the doubts about whether another second-half collapse from the Tom Coughlin Giants was on its way, all of it was hanging in the air inside Ford Field when Jon Kitna let one fly at the two-minute warning. It was 16-10 Giants and if Shaun McDonald could go up and get what would have been a 51-yard touchdown pass, it would have been 17-16 Lions.

"Me and Roy Williams," Sam Madison was saying with a chuckle, "we were standing probably 20 yards from it, and he was telling his guy, 'PLEASE make that play,' and I'm like, 'C'mon Buts, make that play!' "

An unlikely hero named James Butler, a.k.a. Buts, who had lost some playing time to rookie Michael Johnson, made that play, and saved the day.

Jon Kitna would throw a third interception, a deflection off McDonald's hands to Madison, and Big Blue had survived, 16-10. Had survived a season-ending broken left fibula to Mathias Kiwanuka; had survived a second-half hamstring injury to Brandon Jacobs; had survived fumbles in Lions territory from Jacobs and Sinorice Moss; had survived a take-what-they-give-you game [no pass longer than 18 yards to a wide receiver] albeit mistake-free and effi-cient, from Eli Manning; had survived no killer instinct from the offense when it could have killed the clock at the end with one damn first down.

The 6-4 Lions, undefeated at home and filled with bravado, had called this a statement game, but thanks to Butler it was the 7-3 Giants who made the statement. "That we could play with playoff-caliber teams," Madison said. "It's been talked about in the past that we can't win those games, especially on the road as well, we can't win those big games with teams with winning records. Hopefully, we gained a little confidence from this game, and hope-fully it'll help us down the road."

Butler is a 6-foot-3, 215-pound safety from Georgia Tech in his third year as a Giant who has yet to master the art of making reporters wait by his locker until he is completely dressed. "Can you talk while I get dressed, if you don't mind?" he asked.

He was asked about The Pick, his first in 25 games, asked what he was thinking while the ball was in the air.

"I was thinking, 'Why is this ball taking so long to come down?' " he said. "Just trying to make a play on the ball."

Butler, remember, had missed the Miami game (hamstring) in London. "Kitna saw the receiver pass me, so he thought he was open at one point," Butler said.

Justin Tuck had just been called for a ridiculous roughing the passer penalty that left him wondering whether the game is headed towards two-hand touch. "It was actually Cover 2, and they were running deep routes, so it just turned into like, man," Butler said.

Kitna had cut the Lion deficit to 16-10 when Calvin Johnson, who goes 6-foot-5, caught a 35-yard jump ball over Kevin Dockery, who goes 5-foot-8. But in this matchup, Butler had five inches on McDonald.

"He was very short so . . . if he would have caught that ball, y'all would have been all over me right now," Butler said.

Butler, a state triple-jump champion at Bainbridge High in Georgia, looked like Dennis Rodman as he did. "James always is talking about how his vertical [leap] is, so we always clown him about that," Gibril Wilson said.

"He always talks about how he was a basketball star and how he could jump over the rim and do all kinds of dunks and stuff, and it was just good to see him get up. It was pretty much a jump ball, and he came down with th rebound."

"He's always talking about his verti-cal leap and how he can dunk," McQuarters said. "We always tell him we need to see it."

Yesterday, they saw it.

"I'm not a hero," Butler said. He can make that leap if he wants to. ∎

Regular Season • November 25, 2007
Giants 17 • Vikings 41

The Picks

Eli's 4 Interceptions Hand Vikes Victory By Paul Schwartz

There was a moment in the second quarter yesterday when Osi Umenyiora ran off the field to get an intravenous injection and he casually glanced up at the scoreboard. He was shocked by what he saw.

"It was 24-7 and I was like 'How did that happen?' " Umenyiora recalled. It was that sort of now-you-see-it, now-you-don't afternoon for the Giants and especially for Eli Manning. Rarely can one side of the ball, and one player in particular, take a week of game-planning and preparation and render everything utterly useless. Based solely on his performance, the Giants never had a chance. A quarterback can play until he's 50 and never compromise his team's ability to succeed as dreadfully at Manning did, as he threw four interceptions, three of which were returned for touchdowns by the Vikings and another that all but put the Vikes in the end zone.

Each Manning misfire seemed to suck more air out of the rapidly-deflated Giants, who could not come close to overcoming the 28 points Manning handed over in a throwback stinker of a performance that devolved into a ridiculous 41-17 loss at Giants Stadium. "I wish there was some simple explanation for this game but there isn't," a flushed but calm Tom Coughlin said afterward. "We played very, very poorly. You cannot wrap it up and hand it to the guy across the field and we did.

"Obviously I did a very poor job of getting them ready to play." Ready to play is not an apt description of the Giants. Lawrence Tynes sent the opening kickoff rolling out of bounds and two plays later Tarvaris Jackson was burning rookie cornerback Aaron Ross and hitting Sidney Rice on a 60-yard touchdown pass. Ready to play is not an apt description of an offensive line that caved in badly against a Minnesota defensive front not exactly renowned for its ability to rush the passer.

"We were awful," guard Chris Snee said. "I'm embarrassed. We really gave them four touchdowns, which is just unbelievable. I'll be sick all night, probably about it."

Ready to play was not close to an apt description of Manning. No Giants quarterback has ever had three interceptions returned for touchdowns in one game and it hasn't been done in the NFL since 1984. We're talking historic badness here and it came against the NFL's worst-ranked pass defense. "When you throw four interceptions, it is never a good day," said Manning in typical monotone fashion. Manning hit his first three passes and then went 3 of 17 the rest of the first half. On the first interception, Manning misread a hot read and fired over the middle before Jeremy Shockey ever turned around, allowing that old Giants-killer, safety Darren Sharper, to pick the ball off and race 20 yards

(opposite) The latest victim of a Strahan sack: the Vikings' Tarvaris Jackson.

The side-armed Manning threw four interceptions on the day.

for a touchdown. Two years ago, Sharper intercepted Manning three times and had one scoring return in a Vikings upset at Giants Stadium. Trailing 14-7, Manning was backed up in his own territory when he looke over the middle for Plaxico Burress but tossed a terribly off-target pass that safety Dwight Smith hauled in and took to the Giants 8-yard line. On the very next play, three defenders—Justin Tuck, Michael Strahan, and Ross—had a shot at stopping Chester Taylor and none did, as Taylor cruised into the end zone to make it 21-7. The Giants closed to 24-10 early in the third quarter and then allowed Jackson (an efficient 10 of 12 for 129 yards) to run and pass his way on a field goal drive that ate 9:24 off the clock. Early in the fourth quarter, Shockey was free for a potential touchdown but Manning's pass was tipped at the line of scrimmage by defensive end Ray Edwards and deflected into the hands of Smith, who sped 93 yards for what looked to be the most embarrassing touchdown return of the game. But 42 seconds later, linebacker Chad Greenway stepped in front of Shockey and raced 37 yards with the interception to make it 41-10. At 7-4, the Giants have a one-game lead in the NFC Wild Card race but this was no way to dive into a playoff race.

"We always do this, we almost make it hard on ourselves ... the roller coaster goes down and it comes back up," Shockey said. "No, I'm not in shock. We lost a game. No one's going to flip out. We are a good football team, but if we play like that we're not going to win against a high school team." ■

Not All On Eli By Mike Vaccaro

The final indignity, for the quarterback and for the football team, came with three minutes and 47 seconds remaining in one of the most desultory afternoons Giants Stadium has ever seen, fourth down, four yards to go, maybe 4,000 masochists still chained to their chairs at the Meadowlands.

Eli Manning took the snap and was in full retreat at once, looking like Fran Tarkenton in his declining years, doubling back from the oncoming rush, then doubling back again, trying to run away from the Minnesota Vikings and maybe from this full, frightful nightmare of a football game. Twenty-six yards away from the line of scrimmage, the Vikings' Ben Leber finally caught him.

You waited for a good, sustained boo to rain down.

Then realized there weren't enough voices left in the stadium to generate one.

"That, right there, just wasn't meant to be," was how Michael Strahan described the way the Vikings splattered the Giants against their windshield, a 41-17 thrashing that not only sucked the life out of a Thanksgiving Sunday but also put a wicked dent in the season, as well.

It was that bad. It was that unsightly There will be all manner of hand wringing and finger pointing toward No. 10, and there's little doubt that Manning played one of the most egregious games a New York quarterback

has ever played. You can't throw four interceptions, three of them returned for touchdowns, and not draw the lion's share of the loathing.

"I wasn't very good today," Eli said in his standard room-temperature voice.

But this isn't all on the quarterback. This is on everyone. This is on a football team whose fatal flaw remains the same as it's been for far too long, covering far too many seasons: they are far too susceptible to self-congratulation, far too quick to believe their own hype before they're able to generate any real heat.

The Giants won a tough, rugged game in Detroit a week ago, and couldn't have been more pleased with themselves afterward. It was a good win. It wasn't a season-defining win. But they sure did chirp away loudly afterward. And sure seemed awfully proud of themselves.

And sure looked flatter than Kate Moss against the Vikings.

"We just got our butts beaten up out there," running back Reuben Droughn said. "We didn't come out prepared to play."

"It felt lousy out there," safety Gibril Wilson said.

"It was almost comical at times," Strahan said.

No, what's comical was the optimism that elevated the Giants' hubris entering the game, a belief that if Dallas and Green Bay were NFC royalty, then the Giants were just a few steps behind, ready to take their hacks

at the Cowboys and the Packers in January. After all, before yesterday, no one other than the certain No. 1 and No. 2 NFC seeds had beaten them.

The Vikings? They were 4-6. They started a quarterback, Tarvaris Jackson, who has looked barely professional for most of the season. They were coming off a 34-0 smackdown in Green Bay. They were headed toward the kind of oblivion most of the NFC is familiar with.

And positively pummeled the peacockproud Giants.

"Disappointed," Tom Coughlin said, "is not a strong enough word."

Yes: Manning was terrible. He was historically terrible.

But please do not forget the defense, which allowed Jackson to complete a 60-yard scoring pass to Sidney Rice on the second play of the game, which time and again let Jackson escape, which looked thoroughly disinterested in tackling Chester Taylor during his eight-yard scamper that gave the Vikings a 21-7 lead in the second quarter and officially alerted the 78,591 spectators that this was going to be a long, long day.

Do not forget the other members of the offense, which could never establish anything on the ground and dropped half-dozen catchable balls on Manning, all of them before that point in the game when Manning realized the Vikings' fingers were a whole lot sticker than his receivers'.

"This is a team game, and this loss is on the team," Strahan said, correctly. ∎

Regular Season • December 2, 2007
Giants 21 • Bears 16

Giants BEAR-LY Awaken In Time

Late Surge Gives Big Blue A Thrilling Victory In Chicago
By Paul Schwartz

Eli Manning was leading the Giants to ruin. Then he led them to victory. A stunning, improbable victory the Giants needed almost as badly as Manning did. "It wasn't the prettiest . . . at times it was flat-our ugly," Manning said after somehow halting the uproar swirling around him. "But it was sweet." He had thrown two interceptions and lost the ball once on a self-inflicted fumble as the Giants' season was heading down a slippery slope. Based largely on Manning's failings, the Giants trailed virtually all afternoon in the cold, wet, and wind, mired in offensive stagnation. They were down 16-7 in the fourth quarter before Manning shook off the demons that have bedeviled him the past few weeks.

"You got to be able to forget the week before, got to be able to forget the play before and just move on," Manning said. After throwing four interceptions in a terrible loss to the Vikings and laboring mightily for three quarters, Manning led the Giants on a pair of touchdown drives in the final 6:54, then turned the keys to the game over to a resilient defense and, lo and behold, the Giants came back to beat the Bears 21-16 to escape Soldier Field in commanding playoff position.

"He put the bad plays behind him and he realized the game was still to be won on the field," Tom Coughlin said. "He went out and led our team to a win, really a win that I think will give us some inspiration." Why not? At 8-4, the Giants with four games remaining have a working margin over their nearest NFC wild card challengers (Vikings, Lions, and Cardinals, all 6-6) and it would take a total collapse to wind their way out of the postseason. They appeared to be on that path until the unlikely comeback took hold. The Giants, who lost the turnover battle, 4-0, were down 16-7 when Manning lobbed a pass into the end zone not high enough for Plaxico Burress, and cornerback Charles Tillman came up with the interception 13 seconds before the end of the third quarter. The next time Manning got his hands on the ball he misfired on three consecutive passes and trotted off the field after a three-and-out showing no signs of rising out of a month-long funk.

"It looked bleak," Coughlin said. "Our defense kept getting the ball back." Desperation put the Giants in a no-huddle attack and, as it has in the past, that sparked Manning. An 11-play, 75-yard drive cost the Giants running back Derrick Ward (career-high 154 rushing yards) to a broken left leg, but Manning threw low and Amani Toomer scooped the ball off the wet grass for a six-yard scoring play that was initially ruled incomplete and overturned after Coughlin's replay challenge.

"I'm thinking I caught it, there's no way they can not call it a catch," Toomer said. The Giants were within 16-14 with 6:54 remaining, already having put the clamps on return ace Devin Hester, and turned the game over to

(opposite) Derrick Ward eludes Chicago tackles during their early-December matchup.

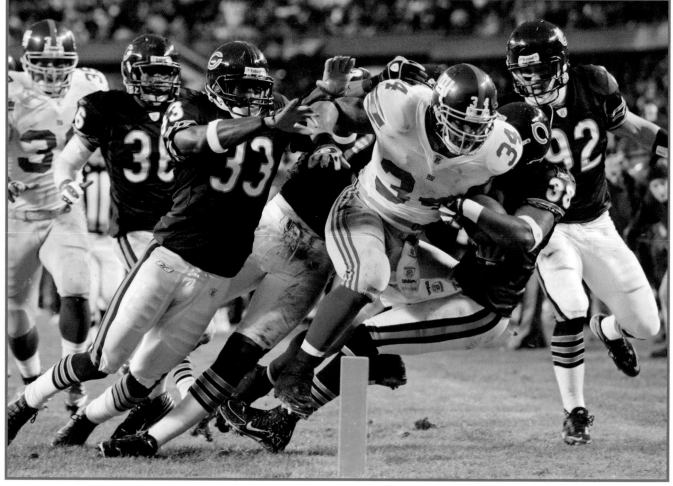

AP/Wide World

Ward leaps for the pylon, but comes up a yard short as the Chicago defense forces him out of bounds.

their defense, which dialed up its sixth sack of Rex Grossman, this one split between Justin Tuck and Kawika Mitchell—who played his best game of the season—to hand Manning the ball on his own 23-yard line with 4:55 left.

"He started off a little shaky but he came through for us," defensive end Osi Umenyiora said. "We knew he was going to come through and he did just that." Manning hit all four of his passes on the final drive, finding little-used David Tyree twice—Tyree's first catches of the season. A 15-yard bullet to Burress put the Giants on the Bears' 2-yard line with 1:37 to go and Coughlin had a decision: Force the Bears to burn their one remaining

time out and kick a field goal or go for the end zone. He opted for the latter and Reuben Droughns scored on first down, with 1:33 remaining. Once again, the defense needed to make a stop. The Bears took over on their 41 after Hester's 19-yard return. They got to the Giants' 28-yard line, but when Grossman's last pass was knocked away by safety James Butler, the Giants exhaled.

"We came into this game looking to be 8-4 and by the grace of God we are," Coughlin said. And by the grace of a Manning-inspired comeback. ■

Eli Finally Shows Some Four-titude

By Steve Serby

Until it became time to win the game, Eli Manning was losing the game again, maybe losing the faith of his team, maybe taking Tom Coughlin and the season down with him.

And then, out of nowhere, under a dark cloud that hung over Soldier Field and seemed to follow this football Charlie Brown, came the compelling, death-defying tale of Dr. Jekyll and Mr. Manning. Out of nowhere, seven minutes from hell, the skittish ugly duckling became an unflappable, beautiful swan.

Out of nowhere, a quarterback who could have passed for Mr. Irrelevant, the last pick of the NFL Draft, became the franchise quarterback who was the first pick of the NFL Draft.

What Manning [16-27, 195 yards] did yesterday, aside from keeping the jackals from pounding on Tom Coughlin's collapsing second-half door, aside from preventing a crisis in confidence for the wild-card race, was save his own hide and reputation, and save himself another hanging in the public square.

It was as if the imposter who had thrown four interceptions against the Vikings and two more against the Bears and lost a fumble had changed in a telephone booth behind the visiting bench.

No, he wasn't more powerful than a locomotive, wasn't able to leap tall buildings in a single bound. All Manning did, down 16-7, was throw for 95 fourth-quarter yards and get his team in the end zone twice and get out alive with a stirring 21-16 comeback victory. "I don't know what that guy's built of, or what he's got inside of him—for all he takes for everything that's been going on these last couple of weeks, I don't know if anybody else can handle the pressure and do what he did the last seven minutes," Antonio Pierc said.

What is it about Dr. Jekyll and Mr. Manning?

"He was bred for this," Pierce said "It's all in his genes. You could look at his demeanor, you could say how he throws the ball . . . but you can't judge his heart and his mentality."

With 6:59 remaining, Manning, third-and-goal at the 6, got some much-needed help when Amani Toomer dove forward to scoop a low throw off the ground to make it 16-14. It was ruled incomplete. Coughlin won the challenge.

"Probably threw a little bit lower than I needed to, but I kinda had to put it out wide," Manning said. Then Big Blue made a big stand.

Manning had one last chance, 4:55 left, at his 23. Manning hit David Tyree for eight yards and a first down. He hit Toomer on a slant for 15 yards. He hit Tyree for 24 yards. At the two-minute warning, he was at the Bear 17.

"People always in the past will talk about his passiveness as weakness and it's completely not," Tyree said. "He's confident in his abilities. He wants to be The Guy on this team and he proved it in the fourth quarter."

Then Eli Cool found Plaxico Burress at the 2, and then Reuben Droughns was in the end zone and it was 21-16 Giants with 1:33 left, and Big Blue slammed the end zone shut on Rex Grossman, just 28 yards away.

Coughlin's offense had been Derrick Ward [24-154, one costly fumble, one season-ending fractured fibula] and a cloud of bust.

Manning, down 16-7, third-and-goal at the 1, spun away from Alex Brown, and lobbed the ball toward the left corner for Burress, but it was underthrown and intercepted by Charles Tillman.

He isn't The Perfect 10. But if you can bloody him, he won't stay down.

"You've gotta be able to forget the week before, you gotta be able to forget the play before and just move on and worry about the next play," Manning said.

Michael Strahan told Manning he was proud of him. "You want a quarterback who's fearless, who's not scared to make mistakes. . . all of us make mistakes," Strahan said. "For Eli to stand up and come back and do those things, hopefully it builds confidence for him."

But you know Manning: Bear today gone tomorrow. ∎

Regular Season • December 9, 2007
Giants 16 • Eagles 13

Birds Get The Boot

Giants Survive A Thrilla In Phila. By Paul Schwartz

As the ball sailed higher and higher into the damp chilled air, one thought raced through the mind of Amani Toomer, the veteran receiver who has been through so many battles eerily similar to this one with the Eagles.

"As it was going up I was thinking 'This game shouldn't be this close, it really shouldn't,' " Toomer said. No matter what the Giants thought, close was where the Giants were, locked in another of those down-and-dirty, inelegant scrums with the hated Eagles. David Akers, whose left foot ended the Giants' season last year, was lined up to try to send yesterday's latest grudge match into overtime. Five seconds remained and the Giants, again making life difficult for themselves, fought back and put the Eagles in a tough spot, needing a 57-yard field goal. Akers hit it clean and true.

"I just prayed as soon as that ball was up, it looked like it had the distance and it was down the middle and it just bowed to the right," Giants rookie safety Craig Dahl said after his first career start. The kick had plenty of distance.

"All I know is the dude booted the hell out of the ball," said linebacker Antonio Pierce, who was not supposed to play, but did. "You could hear it from the sidelines."

"It looked good and we were getting ready to go into overtime."

The ball hooked late and careened off the right upright, halfway up, bouncing harmlessly out of the way as the Giants celebrated a 16-13 victory at Lincoln Financial Field that virtually assures them of their third consecutive NFC playoff appearance.

"All I know is the ball bounced our way," Pierce said. "You can call it whatever you want, just call it a victory." Describe it as the call of the wild (card), as the Giants (9-4) can clinch a playoff spot with a victory Sunday night against the Redskins and even if they don't win another game, have done everything but mathematically seal up a postseason berth. They'll hit the road in the playoffs, and they're 6-1 away from home after another of their typical high-wire road success stories.

"An incredible game and right from the start we knew it was going to be that way," Tom Coughlin said. It didn't have to be that way. The offense, again erratic, hurt itself with two lost fumbles by Brandon Jacobs (he disputed the first), who returned after missing two games with a strained hamstring. The Giants trailed 7-6 at halftime but only by 10-6 in the third quarter after a gallant defensive stand after Jacobs' first fumble handed the Eagles the ball on the Giants' 8-yard line.

Slow-starting Eli Manning—who did not throw an interception in a game for only the second time this season—finally got cooking, uncovering a long-lost big-play target in Plaxico Burress (7-136), who scored the Giants' lone touchdown when Manning correctly diagnosed an all-out

(opposite) Jacobs breaks free from a pair of Eagles tacklers.

Burress shakes out of the grasp of Lito Sheppard en route to a big gain.

blitz and hit Burress on a well executed slant to make it a 13-10 Giants lead. It was 16-10 entering the fourth quarter. The Giants played without their two starting safeties Gibril Wilson and James Butler, and the replacements, rookies, Dahl and Michael Johnson, did not allow a pass play longer than 19 yards. Pierce started despite missing the week of practice with a sprained right ankle and somehow, the defense survived the talents of Brian Westbrook (20-116 rushing, 5-38, 1 TD receiving) and spoiled the return of quarterback Donovan McNabb.

An Akers field goal with 8:36 left cut the Giants' lead to 16-13, but the Giants looked to be sitting pretty when Jacobs rumbled 21 yards to the Philly 5-yard line. Jacobs, though, was stripped of the ball by defensive end Juqua Thomas. The Eagles drove to the Giants' 44-yard line when, on fourth down, McNabb fired to receiver Jason

Avant but Pierce, draped all over Avant, knocked the ball away as the Eagles screamed for pass interference and the Giants took over with 1:57 to go. "The play of the game," defensive end Justin Tuck said. "That's what we come to expect from him. He's our Superman."

The Giants ran the clock down, then the Eagles burned their timeouts and got the ball back on their 11-yard line with 53 seconds left. Three McNabb completions gave Akers one last shot.

"I don't know," said Michael Strahan, when asked about the personality of this Giants team, "but I know it's one that's going to give me a heart attack if we keep winning like this." ∎

Plax-imum Effort By Mike Vaccaro

All time, all motion, all reason seemed to freeze as Eagles kicker David Akers clobbered the football with the side of his left foot, as the ball approached the yellow goal posts, as the 68,594 people inside Lincoln Financial Field unleashed one final roar, as the Giants held their breath on one sideline and the Eagles prepared to explode o the other . . .

Doink!

And then the ball kissed the right upright, and then it tumbled harmlessly to the ground, and silence covered most of Greater Philadelphia, and now it was the Giants who could set their voices free. Most of them, anyway. Plaxico Burress, happy as he was, kept the celebration to a minimum, even as his teammates rejoiced in a game to which he had provided a maximum contribution.

"We always make it harder than it needs to be," Burress would say, much later, after a quick round of postgame treatment on his recalcitrant right ankle, after limping to the podium, after catching seven balls for 136 yards and a touchdown, after providing the most important spark in this workmanlike 16-13 Giants victory that all but salted away the No. 5 seed in the NFC playoffs.

Actually, the degree of difficulty for the Giants shrinks exponentially whenever Burress takes his No. 17 jersey out of the trainer's room—the place where his teammate, Antonio Pierce, has kidded him it belongs—and puts it on his back, with two reasonably func-

tional wheels carrying him along.

Burress has spent almost the entire season nursing that screaming, screeching ankle, and when you see him hobbling across the locker room in his civvies, you wonder how it's even remotely possible for him to have played in all 13 of the Giants' games thus far. Yet that's what he has done. He has only occasionally been a reasonable facsimile of himself, and when he suffers the entire offense bears the consequences

But when he's on . . .

"I always feel if I can get him the ball," Eli Manning said, "he's going to make a play."

"We always feel he can make something happen for us," Tom Coughlin said.

All true. But it's even more than that. Because there are two Elis, and that schizophrenic line is easily drawn: There is the Eli who has Burress as a healthy wingman, and the Eli who doesn't. With Burress, Manning can take a snap, fall down, find his feet, and still deliver a confident throw, as he did late in the second quarter. With Burress, Manning knows he can audible to a play he has just run—as he did on their TD hookup in the third—and know it won't matter because Burress will deliver both of them.

And it's even more than that.

Because there are exactly two reasons why the Giants are able to fancy themselves legitimate players in the NFC. One is their ability to win on the road. Yesterday was their sixth win

away from Giants Stadium in seven games, a victory earned in the midst of the usual cauldron of brotherly Philly warmth—"Lots of one-finger hellos," as Pierce described it—and that's important, because every game the Giant play in the postseason will be outside the 201 area code.

That's a neat skill to own.

But this is a better one: having a gamebreaker, a difference-maker on your roster. And that is Burress' greatest gift to these Giants. As he showed yesterday, he does a couple of things very well, better than any Giants receiver since, maybe, Homer Jones. He knows how to get open. And he knows how to turn a five-yard gain into 10, a 10 yard gain into 20, a first-down catch into a touchdown catch.

In January, that could mean the difference between one-and-done and something else, something different, possibly something awfully special.

It's what allows the Giants to dream big dreams, without making them seem like hallucinations It's what pushes Burress to rehab three times a day, to acupuncture a couple of times a week, to long hours in the trainer's room that, he hopes, will liberate him to the practice field before long.

As Coughlin said wistfully yesterday: "I makes you wonder what [Burress and Eli] could do if they were ever able to practice together."

Maybe. But the evidence of what they're capable of playing games together, real games, is enough to set the imagination soaring. ∎

Regular Season • December 16, 2007
Giants 10 • Redskins 22

Giants Take A' Skin Dive

Shockey Breaks Leg In Ugly Loss By Paul Schwartz

With the Giants seemingly all but assured of a playoff berth, Tom Coughlin last week refused to answer any questions about that impending achievement.

If his team doesn't shape up, Coughlin might be forced to deal with inquiries as to how the Giants played their way out of the playoffs.

"For all the things we did have at stake I just don't think that was our best," Coughlin said last night. Continuing their confounding trend of saving their lousiest performances for their own paying customers, the Giants looked nothing like a playoff-worthy outfit as they were thoroughly outplayed by the Redskins in a 22-10 loss at Giants Stadium that featured more despicable play by Eli Manning.

Adding injury to insult, the Giants suffered a devastating loss, as tight end Jeremy Shockey left early in the third quarter with a fractured left fibula that will keep him out the rest of the season and any postseason games the Giants might have.

Shockey was bent forward by linebacker H.B. Blades before Amani Toomer inadvertently rolled into Shockey's left leg. Shockey will undergo surgery this week. Incredibly, it is the third season-ending fractured fibula to befall the Giants, as linebacker Mathias Kiwanuka and running back Derrick Ward are on injured reserve with identical injuries.

"That's going to be one to the jaw we got to take," running back Brandon Jacobs said.

"To lose Shockey is definitely going to hurt. Not only is he an emotional leader, he makes plays for us," added Michael Strahan. "I know as much of a competitor he is it's really going to kill him to watch."

Just what will Shockey be forced to watch? Will it be a delayed but inevitable playoff clinching or a collapse? At 9-5, the Giants still control their own destiny and can secure a playoff spot Sunday with a victory at Buffalo. If the Giants don't beat the Bills, they might have to beat what likely will be an undefeated Patriots juggernaut in the regular-season finale to clinch a playoff berth. Good luck with that.

"Forget about the playoffs," right tackle Kareem McKenzie said. "Right now it's about playing better football. No way, shape or form we should be performing like this."

The Giants, now a dreary 3-4 at home, followed Manning's lead and wallowed in badness. They never led and rarely looked in synch. Playing amid swirling, gusting wind, Manning' receivers dropped a ghastly 12 passes, a dirty dozen that included five flubs by Jacobs, who might have been wearing oven mitts the way he battered the ball.

(opposite) Manning spies a passing lane through the Washington defense.

"I'm very disappointed; the wind wasn't the best. You just have to concentrate extra hard, and that I didn't do," Jacobs said. "Some of 'em I was able to get my back hand on to them, wasn't able to bring it across. Once you touch it, you should bring it in. I should have had more concentration on the ball."

Manning was a dismal 6 of 21 for 51 yards in the first half, and when his targets weren't dropping the ball, he was often missing them. He finished 18 of 52 for 184 yards and one touchdown. Jacobs ran for 130 yards, but despite the heavy wind the Giants, for some reason, quickly steered away from the ground game. "It's just back to the drawing board," Coughlin said of Manning's recent struggles. "There obviously isn't a simple answer." Somehow, the Giants made a winner of Todd Collins, a career backup who was making his first start at quarterback in 10 years and didn't exactly light it up. Collins completed just eight passes in 25 attempts but made just enough plays and more than Manning.

The Skins, led by Clinton Portis (25-126), ran for 153 yards, the most allowed all season by the Giants defense. Trailing 16-3 at halftime, the Giants looked to make it quitting time as their defense failed to show up to start the second half, allowing the Skins to ramble for a barely contested scoring romp, as Portis ran in to make it 22-3.

Manning finally broke through with a 19-yard touch-

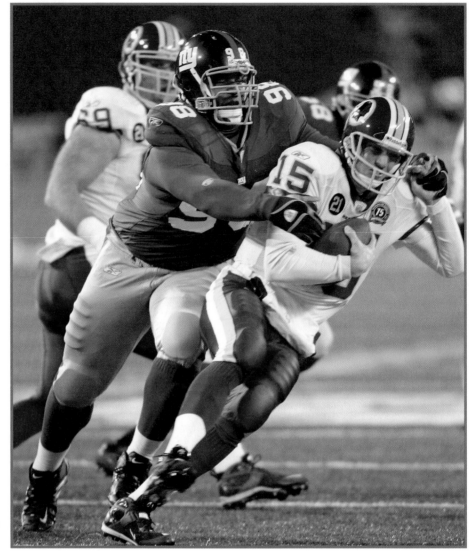

Journeyman Todd Collins is unable to escape the sack by Fred Robbins.

down pass to rookie tight end Kevin Boss with 4:37 left in the third quarter The Giants missed a chance to pull closer when Lawrence Tynes early in the fourth quarter missed a 38-yard field goal attempt.

"We had an opportunity to do it at home and make things a little easy on ourselves, Strahan said, "and we never seem to do that." ■

No Place Like Home For A Big Blue Bust By Mike Vaccaro

The Giants didn't look much like a playoff team across 60 minutes of mostly uninspired football last night at Giants Stadium, an endless exhibition of sloppiness and shoddiness that rendered the stadium a ghost town by 11 o'clock.

They looked like even less of one by the time they staggered back to the locker room after the deflating 22-10 mess was mercifully complete. There, they were greeted with the news that Jeremy Shockey had broken his left leg.

There, they were surely assaulted with the harsh and stinging reality that whatever pretense they had at making serious January noise had ended on this frigid night in East Rutherford. Next year arrived 16 days early in New Jersey.

"There wasn't a lot of good feeling early on that we were doing the things we needed to do," was how Tom Coughlin described it, the coach clearly searching for the most diplomatic way to describe another hometown stinker by his puzzling team.

In the last three games the Giant have played in the shadow of Exit 16W, they have been outclassed by the Cowboys, throttled by the Vikings, and smeared by the Redskins. Not one of those games was even remotely competitive late in the fourth quarter. Are we really supposed to believe that the people who pay to watch these games are more responsible for that than the people who are paid to play them?

"I can't explain it," quarterback Eli Manning said of the Giants' growing home-field futility. "I wish I could."

Too often, what we've seen here is what we saw last night. We saw a defense that allowed far too many big plays, allowed a Redskin journeyman named Todd Collins to riddle them. We saw Manning's happy feet and his none-too-happy pocket presence. We saw receivers drop pass after pass.

And this time, we saw something else, too. We saw Shockey splayed out on the turf, agony etched up and down his limp body. We saw him helped off the field, and carted into the tunnel. And then heard the devastating news: broken leg. Surgery this week. Out for the season.

"It's a terrible thing," Coughlin said, "for him to know he's not going to be here with his teammates at this part of the season."

The Giants losing Shockey isn't exactly the same as the Patriots losing Tom Brady, but it is a reminder of just how slim the Giants' margin for error really is, a reminder of just how ordinary—or worse—the Giants can look when they aren't clicking perfectly.

So instead of wrapping up a playoff berth, the Giants now face two weeks of worry and angst, one game against the Bills in Buffalo and another against the Patriots back at Big Blue's personal theater of pain in the swamp.

Right now, it seems ludicrous to think that just a few days ago, we were wondering if the Giants would have the inclination to want to give the Patriots a full effort in Week 17, if they'd be interested in serving as a 53-man roadblock, a big blue impediment to history.

Now the Giants have to hope they can close out what would be an almost otherworldly 7-1 road record by going into Rich Stadium this Sunday and beating the Bills, whose own playoff aspirations vanished in the snow of Cleveland yesterday. Otherwise, it is entirely possible—given the whims of next week's games and the tiebreakers to follow—that the only small thing separating the Giants from the postseason would be the Patriots.

It's hard to believe. A night that began with snow falling sideways from the sky ended with the Giants walking solemnly from a stadium that was barely a tenth full.

Turns out, they weren't even worth the energy to boot this time. ■

Regular Season • December 23, 2007
Giants 38 • Bills 21

Berth-Day A Giant Bash

Fourth-quarter Burst Earns A Playoff Spot By Paul Schwartz

This is how it had to be for the Giants if they were to somehow, some way, find their way into the playoffs, this imperfect team with a road warrior mentality that makes life so very difficult for themselves and everyone who chooses to pull for them.

These were the Giants, down 14-0 so quickly it hadn't even started raining yet on an afternoon fit for no man to spend outdoors in conditions that deteriorated from harsh to bitter to at times comical in its fury. These were the Giants, with quarterback Eli Manning fumbling five times and turning the ball over four times, finally realizing if they were to win on this terrible day they would have to hitch up their pants, strap on their helmets and simply run the football either into the playoffs or into infamy.

"That is what you do in conditions like that," running back Brandon Jacobs said. "You run the ball." They ran the ball. Punishing and pulverizing with Jacobs, darting and dynamic with a rookie named Ahmad Bradshaw who enjoyed his NFL coming-out party. There was a defensive spark—make that an ignition—by a hardworking linebacker, Kawika Mitchell, who returned an interception 20 yards for a touchdown, and a fourth quarter barrage was on. And then, when the Giants were finished seemingly invading the end zone at will, after they doused an already saturated Tom Coughlin with a mixture of Gatorade and ice, they finally were allowed to come inside, earning for the third consecutive season a

playoff berth, this one courtesy of a wet and wild 38-21 victory that had to be seen to be believed.

"It meant a lot to us to win this game and get into the playoffs," receiver Amani Toomer said. "We are not ever going to quit. We're always fighting to the end." The end is not near for the Giants (10-5), who clinched an NFC wild card berth and now have the luxury of playing Saturday night's regular-season finale against the 15-0 Patriots any way they see fit, with no pressure strings attached. Passing the ball was treachery in winds of 23 miles an hour that gusted to 36 mph, in temperatures that started out at 52 degrees at kickoff but rapidly plummeted, in rain that started slowly and then blew in off Lake Erie in torrents and then changed into sleet and then snow at Ralph Wilson Stadium. All 59 points in the game were scored going into the east end zone.

"It kind of felt like the Forrest Gump movie, where the rain's coming sideways, even coming from underneath sometimes," center Shaun O'Hara said. It was a day to play it safe and, after some prodding, that's what the Giants did, amassing a season-high 291 rushing yards nearly split evenly between Bradshaw (17-151, including an 88-yard touchdown for a team rookie record) and Jacobs (24 carries for a career-high 145 yards and two

(opposite) Jacobs plows through the snow shower and the Bills defense to score a touchdown.

Strong blocking opens a big hole for Jacobs to rumble through.

TDs before leaving with a sprained left ankle).

The Giants righted the ship with 17 second quarter points on two Jacobs touchdowns—the second on a career-high 43 yard run—but Manning, working against the wind, on the first play of the third quarter threw behind Plaxico Burress and was intercepted by linebacker Keith Ellison. That led to a Marshawn Lynch touchdown 66 seconds into the second half for a 21-17 Bills lead. After that, of the Giants' next 19 plays in the quarter, 18 were runs and just one a pass. In the second half, Manning (7 of 15, 11 yards, 2 INTs) threw the ball three times; the Giants ran it 31 times for 208 yards.

"Run, run after run after run, really putting it on us to get the job done," guard Chris Snee said. "We came through."

Mitchell, in the first minute of the fourth quarter, intercepted Trent Edwards and took it to the house to put the Giants up for good, 24-21, and Bradshaw, from the Giants 12-yard line on a play called 38 Power, told his linemen if they blocked it right he'd score. They did and he did. Corey Webster, salvaged from the scrap heap, took back an interception 34 yards and before long Coughlin was getting doused not once, but twice.

"It was the chunks of ice that gave me some mixed thoughts about exactly what the intention was there," Coughlin said, attracting laughter as he broke into a smile. ■

Coughlin: From Thin Ice To Icing It In One Season By Steve Serby

He was everybody's favorite lame duck in the summer, after a season when too many viewed him as The Ugly Duckling. But late yesterday, doused by his playoff-bound Giants in ice water in what felt like the frozen tundra of upstate New York, Tom Coughlin had turned into a beautiful, albeit wet, swan.

He doesn't have a perfect team, but the Giants are fighters, which means they are now a reflection of their head coach.

"I would say so," Antonio Pierce said after Giants 38, Bills 21. "The guy's gotten in a better mood . . . he's more personable. . . . The guy walked in the meeting room for the first time after a loss with a smile. Wednesday. Shocking. Shocking. Probably one of the most shocking things I've ever seen in my life."

Coughlin didn't know whether to laugh or cry when Pierce and Michael Strahan got him with one cooler, and Osi Umenyiora and Justin Tuck got him with another.

"He seemed a little upset at first and then he started laughing," Umenyiora said. "He smiled," Pierce said, and then chuckled. "I don't know if he smiled 'cause he was freezing his [butt] off."

"It was the chunks of ice that gave me some mixed thoughts about exactly what the intention was there . . . it was a little chilly," Coughlin said.

He sold them talk is cheap, play the game, and they bought it.

"It's been a team, it's been a group of guys that from Day 1 have bought into the total team concept," Coughlin said. "They fought for each other, they supported one another, they believe in one another. I think it's group of guys that really believe that together-we-are-one kinda theme that we've talked about all year long."

"We have a great sense o unity right now," Kawika Mitchell said. Down 14-0, Coughlin continue to run the ball down Buffalo's throat with Brandon Jacobs and Ahmad Bradshaw.

"It was a game we knew we had to win, and as I told the players last night, it says something about an individual, about a team, when they know that they have the opportunity to secure a spot in the playoffs and that we're on the road again; we've had a lot of success on the road this year, and we played our way through some adversity . . . I was glad to see us get our 10th win and secure our spot in the playoffs," Coughlin said.

He poked fun at himself.

"I thought the second quarter was really the momentum quarter for us . . . when I first looked out there at the start of the second quarter, the rain was going sideways, so even I could figure out that we had the wind at our back there in the second quarter," Coughlin said.

The 15-0 Patriots are next. Will Coughlin play it to win or rest some starters?

"The team that we're playing, they'll have to give some thought to that as well," Coughlin said. "We'll see. First I'll gather all the medical information at the start of the week and then I'll make some decisions on that."

Coughlin is the first Giants coach to reach the playoffs three straight times since Bill Parcells did it from 1984-86. Did yesterday ensure that he'll be back?

"That's not appropriate to talk about right now," GM Jerry Reese said. "All that will take care of itself."

Coughlin took a team no one imagined could make the playoffs and got them there. He deserves to be back. ■

Regular Season • December 29, 2007
Giants 35 • Patriots 38

Sweat 16 For Perfect Pats

Pats Cap Unbeaten Season—But Giants Put Scare In'Em
By Paul Schwartz

Once the competitive juices started flowing, the Giants were incapable of stopping the torrent from overtaking their emotions. They were locked in an intense, combative game with the unbeaten Patriots, taking it to them and loving every minute of it. "To be honest, once [Giant coach Tom Coughlin] put us out there I doubt anyone would come out," linebacker Antonio Pierce said. "We had a chance to make history."

The Giants did not make history, nor did they prevent the Patriots from moving inexorably closer to perfection. But they came so close.

"There's nothing but positives," Coughlin said. "I don't have any negatives about this game. We had everything to gain and nothing to lose." That's an astounding remark from the coach after a 38-35 loss at pumped-up Giants Stadium, further evidence of the uniqueness and strangeness of an evening where the regular season came to an end.

Early in the third quarter of a game fueled by immense hype, the Giants led 28-16, giving the mighty Patriots all they could handle. The scent of an upset, though, only served to empower the Pats, who leaned on the brilliance of Tom Brady and Randy Moss to score the next 22 points to escape with their prize intact. The Patriots became the first team in NFL history to finish a regular season with a 16-0 record and the fourth to go unbeaten in regular season, the most recent being the 1972 Dolphins.

Next up for the Pats on their path to perfection is matching the '72 Dolphins by sweeping through the playoffs and winning the Super Bowl, which would allow Bill Belichick's marauders to stake a claim as the greatest team of all time.

This was a spirited and at times uplifting playoff primer for the Giants, who next weekend face the Buccaneers in an NFC wild-card game in Tampa. Eli Manning, in a performance he can build on, tossed four touchdown passes—two to Plaxico Burress—and, enjoying the moderate temperature and lack of wind, played better than he has in months.

"I don't know of any better way to prepare for the playoffs," Coughlin said. "This is the momentum, if you will, we were looking forward to." Coughlin and Pierce pointed to the closeness of the game as reason for great encouragement—"We didn't get blown out and we covered the spread," Pierce said—but others took no solace in battling the Pats to the wire. "I didn't learn anything new. ... I knew we could compete with them," receiver Amani Toomer said. "We didn't do much of anything. We lost."

Manning's three-yard scoring pass to Burress with 1:04 remaining pulled the Giants within three points, but they failed to recover the onside kick, ending their gallant upset bid.

As promised, Coughlin put all his starters on the field,

(opposite) Jacobs breaks free for a big gain against the Patriots.

Teammates congratulate Jacobs on his touchdown run that opened the scoring.

determined to go at the Pats as hard as possible for as long as possible before resting some of his key players. He kept his starters on the field the whole way. The hope was that the Giants could compete and remain healthy, but they were not that fortunate. Kawika Mitchell, the valuable weak side linebacker, went down in the first quarter with a sprained knee and was not able to return.

In the second quarter, center Shaun O'Hara limped off with a sprained knee. In the fourth quarter, veteran cornerback Sam Madison exited with an abdominal strain.

At times, it was hard to believe what was transpiring out on the turf. The Giants led 21-16 at halftime and then extended the lead when Manning tossed what might be the best pass he's thrown this season, rolling to his right, pump-faking and drilling a 19-yard rope that Burress hauled in while dragging his feet along the right side of

the end zone. That made it 28-16 with 9:12 left in the third quarter. Game most certainly on. That storyline was not to the Patriots' liking, and they marched 73 yards, with Laurence Maroney scoring from six yards out to narrow the deficit to 28-23.

It was a game effort from the Giants but they faded down the stretch. Brady (32 of 42, 35 yards, 2 TDs) was basically unstoppable, as was receiver Wes Welker (11-122).

Brady, with 11:06 remaining, heaved the football as far as he could, and Moss, on a busted coverage, simply ran past safety James Butler for an easy 65-yard scoring play, putting New England up for good, 31-28, after a successful two-point conversion run by Maroney. ∎

Pats Pull One Out Of Their Asterisk

By Mike Vaccaro

There were 35 seconds left when Tom Brady's knee touched the Giants Stadium turf for the final time, and by then the headsets were off the coaches and the inhibitions had all left the players. The Patriots were 30 seconds away . . . 25 . . . 20 . . . from doing what no team has ever done, winning a 16th regular season game.

Bill Belichick started to take the long walk across the field. On other occasions, after other games on this field, his every step has been scrutinized and monitored and analyzed, because headed the other way was Eric Mangini, once his mentor now his nemesis, once his friend and now a deeply-rooted adversary. Fifteen seconds were left . . . 10 . . . 5.

This time, it was Tom Coughlin walking toward him, and so this time there were smiles on either end, and good feeling, and good tidings. Once upon a time, Belichick and Coughlin worked together, on the same Bil Parcells staff, and they won themselves a Super Bowl together

"Great job," Coughlin said.

"Good luck," Belichick said.

Now the time was gone and the game was over, a 38-35 win for the Patriots in which they needed every ounce of their talent and every drop of their guile and their guts to get to 16-0. The Giants hit them with a quick first-quarter punch, got knocked down themselves, kept coming after them,

held a 28-16 advantage in the third quarter, still held a lead in the fourth.

"The Giants are a very good team," Belichick said. "They're a playoff team, and they showed why tonight." But the Patriots are a forever team, a team playing for its place in history, and they showed why last night, too. They elicit so many different emotions in so many different people. The hoodie has become a sinister fashion staple. The asterisk we've displayed all year long in this newspaper has been an interesting talking point. It drives Patriots fans insane. It makes fans of other teams cackle.

Caught cheating?

Sure they were. They were caught. They paid their debt. And have spent the first 17 weeks of this football season trying to chisel the asterisk away. They have been dominant a lot of the time. They have been down, and found ways to get back up. The Colts had them beat; the Pats came back. The Eagles kept digging uppercuts into their ribs. The survived. The Ravens were one play away from kneecapping them; that play never happened.

And now, on the final Saturday night before the final Sunday of the season, the Giants got after them hard, got after them good, got after them right from the start. Eli Manning was terrific. Brandon Jacobs was tremendous. The stadium, which from the sound of things this week was supposed to become a cross between Faneuil Hall

and Fenway Park, was a Giants stadium the whole way, the whole night.

"This," said Plaxico Burress, recipient of two touchdown passes, "was what I expected the New York Giants to be like all year."

This, however, is what the New England Patriots have been like all year. They wait you out. They smoke you out. Then they pounce. With 11:25 to play in the game, trailing 28-23, Tom Brady finally aired one out, to where Randy Moss was standing wide open, alone after Giants safety Gibril Wilson had fallen down. Brady, for one of about six times all year, underthrew the ball.

"I needed some redemption," he would say.

It wasn't the same play. It wasn't the same route. But it was damn close enough. The very next play, there was Brady crow-hopping in the pocket, unleashing another perfect parabola. And there was Moss, who was even more open this time even though nobody had fallen down, same part of the field, running under Brady's bomb like Willie Mays at the Polo Grounds.

The Giants lead was gone. The Meadowland was silent, save for those vibrant cells of Stub-Hub customers wearing Pats gear. There was still plenty of football game left. But the Patriots weren't going to lose now, not against these 2007 Giants, not if the '86 Giants had come out of the tunnel to help, backed up by the '72 Dolphins. ∎

Ahmad Bradshaw takes a handoff from Manning.

Playoffs • January 6, 2008
Giants 24 • Buccaneers 14

Kick The Buc-ket

Eli Torches Tampa, Sets Up Third Date With Dallas
By Paul Schwartz

One by one, the Giants raced off the field at Raymond James Stadium, their feet barely touching the ground, but Amani Toomer, the veteran receiver, would not go quietly. "He can be had!" Toomer shouted. "HE CAN BE HAD!"

The he, of course, is Eli Manning and yesterday he could not be had, not by cornerback Ronde Barber (who made that bold claim) and the Buccaneers defense, not by any of his many critics. On a warm and blue-skied afternoon majestically fit for the Florida outdoors, Manning played a near-flawless game and his teammates followed suit, replacing a shaky first quarter with rock-solid dominance.

By the time Manning was finished carving through the NFL's best pass defense and his pass-rushing mates were through pounding Jeff Garcia into the dirt, the Giants erased the memories of their past postseason failures with a resounding 24-14 trouncing of the Buccaneers and their quarterback more than anyone led the charge.

"If he keeps on playing like that," Plaxico Burress said, "we can win a lot more ballgames."

There indeed is another ballgame for the Giants (11-6), who head to Dallas freshly installed as a 7.5-point underdog for Sunday's NFC divisional playoff game against the top-seeded Cowboys, who beat the Giants twice this season. It's on the road again, where the Giants are now 8-1.

"It's a great feeling but you can't just be content with this," an ebullient (for him) Manning said. "You have to win the first one to keep this going. It's about keeping this going further in the playoffs."

Manning's first playoff victory after losses the past two seasons—and the first for the Giants since they made it to the Super Bowl following the 2000 season—turned into a clinic in how to win this time of year. Manning (20 of 27, 185 yards, two touchdowns) did not come close to a single turnover and compiled a sterling quarterback rating of 117.1. He kept the ball moving on slants and pumpfakes and dump-offs with numbing efficiency as the Giants shrugged off a 7-0 first-quarter deficit with 24 unanswered points.

There were heroes galore. Toomer (7-74) hauled in one of Manning's scoring passes and Brandon Jacobs plowed in with another. Grey Ruegamer started at center in place of injured Shaun O'Hara with no discernable drop-off. The Giants sacked Garcia only once but hit him with punching-bag regularity. "It wears on you, it does," the 37-year old Garcia wearily admitted.

And then there was Corey Webster, the third-year cornerback whose career had regressed as he was relegated to the bench. Stepping in for injured Sam

(opposite) Manning throws for a fourth quarter touchdown against Tampa.

Steve Smith goes down, but not before a long gain.

Madison, Webster not only started for the first time since the first month of the season but actually was assigned to shadow Joey Galloway, the Bucs speedy deep threat. Galloway finished with one catch for nine yards. Webster finished with one interception, one huge fumble recovery on special teams and, perhaps, a career-saving performance.

"I just wanted to rise up to the occasion and I think I did a pretty good job," Webster said.

Manning got off to a slow start as the Giants went three-and-out on their first two series. Trailing 7-0, an offensive adjustment made all the difference. With the Bucs putting eight defenders in the box, leaving Toomer and Burress in single coverage and daring Manning to beat them with his arm, the Giants turned their quarterback loose with short passes designed to soften the Tampa defense.

Amani Toomer celebrates the defense's takeaway that sealed the Giants' first round win.

A 5-yard flip to Jacobs made it 7-7. After Michael Strahan came up with a sack of Garcia the Giants got the ball back and rookie Ahmad Bradshaw immediately injected a spark with a nine-yard run and another rookie, Steve Smith, had a 21-yard catch-and-run after a strong Manning pump-fake. Jacobs slipped a tackle try by Ryan Sims and it was Giants 14-7.

Micheal Spurlock fumbled the opening kickoff of the second half after a strip by Tank Daniels, leading to a Lawrence Tynes field goal. On the signature drive of the game, the Giants in 15 plays ate up 8:37 bridging the third and fourth quarters, moving 92 yards, capped when the cagey Toomer slipped free for a 4-yard scoring pass with 8:03 remaining to seal the deal.

"We have good character on our team, and we have toughness," said Tom Coughlin, whose future employment with the Giants is assured.

The words during the week from Barber—Tiki's identical twin brother—who told *The Post* that Manning's inconsistency meant he "could be had" rang hollow on this day. Barber willingly gave Eli credit. "He played great," Barber said.

"It seems," crowed Burress, "like he had their number today." ∎

Final-E! E-fficient Eli Just Couldn't Be Had By Steve Serby

This was, in so many ways, the kid's E-MANNcipation Proclamation, the day Eli Manning stood up and announced: Why not me? Why can't I take my team to the Super Bowl?

It was the day he won a playoff game, the third time the charm, and freed himself, and Tom Coughlin, from the big-game shackles that had kept the two of them chained far, far away from New York's unrequited love.

Final-E.

Manning (20-27, 185 yards, 2 touchdowns) wasn't Phil Simms in Pasadena, but close enough. He never cracked, never made one of those mind-blowing mistakes, never stopped being the calm, cool field general who kept his team believing.

And when Giants 24, Bucs 14 was over, No. 10 was thinking 10-gallon bigger. "It's not gonna be easy, we got a tough challenge against Dallas, we know that, we played 'em twice this year. . . . But, I think third time could be a charm," Manning said.

Jaws dropped, and someone asked, half-kiddingly: "Does that mean you're guaranteeing a victory?"

Manning smiled and said, "No more stupid questions, please."

And everyone in the interview room laughed.

His older brother Cooper Manning had been standing proudly next to him in the locker room.

"Congratulations, I'm proud of you," Cooper said.

"Fun day out there," Eli said.

Cooper was asked if he was as happy for Eli, the baby brother, as he was for Peyton the night he won the Super Bowl. "It's baby steps," Cooper said. "Every time you do something for the first time, it's pretty special."

For Coughlin, it was a validation of his decision to play to win against the Patriots. It was a triumph that epitomized the very essence of team . . . a tough, prideful, resilient team . . . but more than anyone, it was Manning who rose up from the ashes of mediocrity and grabbed the moment by the throat.

"It was a monkey off the back for the whole team, but I think especially for him," Antonio Pierce said. "When you see your guy that's been criticized all year, and the media's been on him tough and everybody thinks he can't handle the pressure, he constantly keeps proving that he can."

"Everybody says, 'Oh, he doesn't have the fire,' whatever, but there's more than one way to lead a team, and he showed it today," Amani Toomer said. "You don't have to be a

rah rah guy to get people to respect you, and everybody on our team definitely respects him a lot."

The piece de resistance was the 15-play, 92-yard, 8:37 touchdown drive that started near the end of the third quarter and broke the Bucs' will. It culminated in a 4-yard touchdown pass to Toomer on third-and-goal. "I pumped inside to Kevin Boss, got Ronde to cheat in just a little bit, and Amani Toomer did a great job of just finding the open lane and making a tough catch," Manning said. "It was a big-time drive."

The Giants trailed 7-0 when Manning, much more Montana than Marino, accepted the mantle of franchise quarterback.

Much more E-fficient (no pass longer than 21 yards) than E-lectric.

"It doesn't make a difference to me what a player says, or what anyone says," Manning said. "It doesn't make me attack him any more or go after him or do anything different."

He couldn't be had. Final-E. ■

Jacobs barrels his way to a second quarter touchdown.

Playoffs • January 13, 2008
Giants 21 • Cowboys 17

'Boys Buried By Big Blue

Giants Pack Their Bags For Green Bay By Paul Schwartz

As the final in what was a legion of heroes, a vet named R.W. McQuarters, came down with the football in the end zone for the interception heard 'round the Giants football world, an exhale of such immense proportions blew all the way to, well, frigid Green Bay.

That's where the Giants, incredibly and improbably, are headed to compete in an NFC Championship game most onlookers believed they'd get only as close to as their bigscreen plasma televisions.

The season lives on, breathing and vibrant, after an emotional and tense and relentless and exhausting evening last night battling from ahead and then behind and then ahead again and, ultimately, staring down the rival Cowboys and Tony Romo, firing desperately to his array of star-studded weapons, seeking to pick apart a depleted and no-name defensive secondary, hoping to send a dagger into this incredible upset the Giants were fashioning.

And then, it was over. Romo on fourth down, 23 yards from the touchdown he and the Cowboys needed and the Giants were hell-bent to prevent, looked deep for Terry Glenn, singled up with McQuarters, another of those many fill-ins forced to join in on this day. There were nine seconds left when McQuarters came down with the ball and the Giants had a 21-17 victory at Texas Stadium in an NFC Divisional playoff game that was as

riveting as most any you're about to see.

"I ain't never wanted to cry in football before but that was the best moment I ever had in football," linebacker Antonio Pierce said.

Save the tears and pass the ear-warmers. The Giants, winners of a franchise-record nine consecutive road games, on Sunday face Brett Favre and the Packers at historic Lambeau Field—game-time temperature is expected to be 11 degrees, or colder—in the NFC Championship game for the right to represent the conference in Super Bowl XLII in sunny Glendale, Arizona.

"It's a little premature to be saying the 'SB' word," center Shaun O'Hara said.

"We'll be an underdog, we'll be the worst team in the NFC Championship history and we'll be happy about it," added guard Chris Snee, whose club is 7-point underdogs. "We'll go in there and we'll fight to the end."

Doubt them at your own risk. This was to be the year of the Cowboys, the No. 1 seed in the NFC, primed and ready but now done and done and the Giants were thrilled to be the team to keep them home. After losing two games during the regular season to the Cowboys, the Giants heard all week why they could not win and then fumed in silence as a mouthy receiver named Patrick Crayton accused them of talking too much to hide the

(opposite) Manning throws for a first half touchdown in Dallas.

R.W. McQuarters eludes tacklers on a punt return.

fact they were scared of the Cowboys.

Then the Giants (12-6) took to the field, took a 7-0 lead on Eli Manning's 52-yard catch-and-run touchdown hookup to Amani Toomer slightly more than three minutes into the game, and settled in for a titanic struggle.

With Manning maturing by the minute, the Giants took the lead for good on a Brandon Jacobs one-yard plunge with 13:29 remaining and then held off the Cowboys, Romo, and Terrell Owens once, twice, three times, forcing Owens to tears and leaving the Cowboys (13-4) still searching for their first playoff win since 1996.

"Patrick Crayton, I'll see you next year," said Jacobs, the primary object of Crayton's verbal abuse.

"You know what, I can't say that we love them and they love us," added Michael Strahan. "I hope T.O. has his popcorn ready, maybe he and Crayton can sit in his home theater and watch us next week."

So much could have gone wrong. A defensive backfield playing without a starting cornerback (Sam Madison) and its nickel back (Kevin Dockery) lost another corner, rookie Aaron Ross, in the third quarter to a dislocated shoulder. There were problems hauling down Marion Barber (27-129) and trouble corralling Romo. And the defense could not get off the field.

After Romo hit Owens—playing despite a high left ankle sprain—on a 5-yard scoring pass on the first play of the second quarter, the Cowboys embarked on a gargantuan 20-play, 90-yard drive that took 10:28 off the clock, culminated in Barber's 1-yard touchdown run, and left the Giants trailing 14-7 just 47 seconds before halftime when Manning finally got to touch the ball on his 29-yard line.

"We weren't going to take a knee," Manning said.

No, they weren't. Manning in seven plays and a mere 47 seconds got the Giants even on Toomer's second TD grab, a huge momentum boost going into the half.

Nick Folk's 34-yard field goal midway through the third quarter put the Cowboys ahead 17-14 but a 25-yard

Strahan celebrates the win that sent the Giants to Green Bay and the NFC Championship game.

punt return by McQuarters set in motion the game-winning drive, followed by a game-saving defensive stand.

"I am so proud of our players, they really rose up," Tom Coughlin said.

"They were expecting us to roll over, I think they underestimated us, I don't think they respected us," added an elated Toomer.

And now, Green Bay.

"Words cannot describe," left tackle David Diehl gushed, "how awesome that will be." ■

Blue-'D'-ful Day By Steve Serby

On the sidelines now, after an improbable hero named R.W. McQuarters had intercepted Tony Romo in the end zone on fourth-and-11, fourth-and-season from the Giants 23, the All-Joes who had delivered a ten-gallon doomsday to all the All-Pros erupted in a Deja Blue euphoria that the underdog 1990 Giants who swaggered into Candlestick and denied Joe Montana a threepeat would have recognized.

"Getcha popcorn ready," the Giants roared. "We're going to Green Bay!"

There were nine seconds left when Eli Manning took a knee inside a hushed Texas Stadium and in the visiting locker room, 60 minutes from the Super Bowl, one of the toughest, grittiest Giant teams in memory acted like children.

"You couldn't hear," Antonio Pierce said. "It was too many people yelling —from the owners to the head coach to our quarterback."

And what were they yelling?

"HOW 'BOUT THEM GIANTS!" Pierce said. "HOW 'BOUT THEM GIANTS!"

There is no crying in football, but Pierce broke the rule. "Best moment I ever had in football," Pierce said.

This was the time and this was the place for them to remember that defense wins championships. Big D in Dallas meant them.

Aaron Ross was on the sidelines with a bum shoulder, which meant the Giants were down to three cornerbacks, and one of them was a rookie free agent from Howard named Geoffrey Pope.

No matter. No excuses. You finish the job, and you show you belong in the NFC Championship game.

On third down, Romo, buying time all day to escape a savage pass rush as only he can, had tried for Patrick Crayton in the right corner of the end zone, against Corey Webster, incomplete.

In the huddle, McQuarters said:

"Keep 'em out of the end zone." It was Pierce, the heart and soul middle linebacker whose shoulder chip grows bigger with every slight, who was doing most of the talking.

"As fast as I can talk, I read everything off that I remembered that everybody said about us this week," Pierce said. "That's why my heart's still goin' about a buck-fifty."

This was an hour after Giants 21, Cowboys 17. "Trust me, I almost said close to a thousand words in 30 seconds," Pierce said.

Romo, from the shotgun, didn't look for Terrell Owens. He looked for Terry Glenn, back from a season-long knee injury, lined up in the slot against McQuarters.

"Terry Glenn sorta ran like a skinny post and he was sorta bending it across the end zone," McQuarters said. "We had a defense called, and I had inside leverage, and I wanted to make sure that he declared his route first, and I was able to get my head around and get my hands up in time."

He is a journeyman who has bounced around the league to get to this moment, 60 minutes from the Super Bowl.

"Hey man, this is my 10th year in the league, this is my third time making the playoffs, this is my first time going to the NFC Championship . . . it's just a great feeling, man," McQuarters said.

Third time's a charm indeed. "This team never stopped comin'," Pierce said.

"At this point," a joyous John Mara said, "anything is possible."

It wasn't lost on Pierce that Jerry Jones handed out two tickets Friday to his Cowboys for the NFC Championship game, and how sweet it was to shut Patrick Crayton up.

"We got the butter for the popcorn and the salt for him; he was a little salty towards us for some odd reason," Pierce said.

HOW 'BOUT THEM GIANTS! ∎

Playoffs • January 20, 2008
Giants 23 • Packers 20

3rd Tynes A Charm!!

Kicker Caps Super Bowl Run With OT Kick By Paul Schwartz

Nothing deters these Giants. Nothing stops these Giants. Not unholy cold. Not the mystique of sacred Lambeau Field or the presence of future Hall of Fame quarterback Brett Favre or yet another road game they were supposed to lose or more than 60 minutes of what seemed to be dominating play that was headed toward to nothing but heartache.

And certainly not the need for retribution on a historic night when heroes and villains intermingled until finally, ultimately, a kicker named Lawrence Tynes who had caused so much angst allowed the Giants to erupt in jubilation and exultation with a boot that somehow, some way, sends them to a truly improbable trip to the Super Bowl.

This is the stuff of dreams.

"Not in this weather, not from that distance and not at Lambeau Field," Tynes exclaimed afterward.

It was Tynes who on the final play of regulation in the NFC Championship Game against the favored Packers could not recover from the high snap of rookie Jay Alford and sent a potential game-winning 36-yard field goal attempt knuckling wide left. And then, after an interception of Favre by a cornerback named Corey Webster—thirsting for retribution after a blown play earlier in the night—who set Tynes up again, this time with a tough 47-yard field goal just 2:35 into overtime. Tynes thrust himself into Giants lore with a kick that was straight and true and then sprinted for the tunnel, knowing the Giants had beaten the Packers 23-20 and were on their way to

sunny Glendale, Arizona, for a Super Bowl XLII date with the mighty and unbeaten Patriots.

Of course, the Giants are 13-point underdogs.

"It was beautiful—Ice Bowl II, with a different ending," linebacker Antonio Pierce said. "A New York ending! Beautiful."

It was the longest postseason field goal ever at Lambeau and Tynes' right foot was black and blue from the strain of striking a frozen football. Time will likely judge this game fondly, as it was contested in the most bitter of conditions (minus-one degree on the thermometer, minus-23 wind chill factor), the second-coldest game at Lambeau.

"I can't describe how bad it was," Toomer said. "Breathing in the air would burn your lungs and it was just ridiculous." Incredibly, these teams battled through the elements and produced an electrifying game that ebbed back and forth, with the Giants dominating everything in terms of total yardage and time of possession but unable to build any real lead. Eli Manning outplayed Favre, Plaxico Burress (11-154) overwhelmed cornerback Al Harris and the Giants (13-6) continued their uncanny ability to send opposing fans home miserable with their 10th consecutive road victory, their third in this wild playoff run.

The Giants squandered chances in the red zone and took a 6-0 lead on a pair of Tynes field goals but Favre on

(opposite) Manning raises his arms in celebration after Bradshaw's third quarter touchdown run.

Manning audibles at the line in the face of the Green Bay defense.

Strahan and Madison Hedgecock celebrate the win and the upcoming trip to Arizona and Super Bowl XLII.

one play got the Packers (14-4) on top, as Webster slipped and Donald Driver raced with a 90-yard catch-and-run touchdown pass play. The Packers led 10-6 at halftime. Four Green Bay penalties helped a drive that ended with a Brandon Jacobs scoring burst to put the Giants ahead 13-10. A personal foul penalty on Sam Madison led to a touchdown grab for Donald Lee to put the Packers up 17-13. Back and forth it went, a battle in the tundra.

A 33-yard kickoff return by Domenik Hixon paved the way for a four-yard touchdown scamper by rookie Ahmad Bradshaw, putting the Giants up 20-17 late in the third quarter. Cornerback R.W. McQuarters intercepted Favre but fumbled on the return and Mason Crosby hit a field goal to tie the game at 20.

Tynes with 6:49 left in regulation missed on a 43-yard field goal try and the bundled crowd roared in approval. Bradshaw ran 48 yards for an apparent touchdown but it was called back by a holding penalty on guard Chris Snee. Manning got Tynes in position for the game-winner but he missed.

Then came overtime, the Giants lost the toss and Favre got the ball.

"That's what we wanted, trust me," Pierce said.

Soon enough, the defense got the ball back to Manning and Manning gave Tynes another shot and his kick sent the Giants to the Super Bowl.

"That was some game," said Tom Coughlin, his face red from the bitter cold but unable to contain a wide smile as he heads to his first Super Bowl. "I think the thing I am most proud of about this team is the way they hang together, the way they played hard." ■

Giants Know What It Takes To Beat Pats
By Paul Schwartz

The Giants were swept in the two-game regular season series against the Cowboys and then knocked them out of the playoffs.

The Giants in the second game of the season faltered in the fourth quarter of a 35-13 loss to the Packers and last night knocked the Packers out of the playoffs with a 23-20 overtime victory in the NFC Championship Game at Lambeau Field.

The Giants in the regular-season finale decided to go for broke and not rest anyone, even with the playoffs already clinched, and they put on a thrilling display in a 38-35 loss to the Patriots in a game that catapulted Eli Manning's confidence and sent the Giants into the postseason in a good frame of mind.

This retribution tour continues.

The Giants on February 3 face the unbeaten Patriots in Super Bowl XLII in Glendale, Arizona, once again looking to beat a team that beat them the first time around.

"We know what it takes to beat 'em," Manning said.

"We wouldn't want it any other way," added center Shaun O'Hara. "At least now we know nobody can pick us."

No doubt, the Giants will be the "other" team for the week out west.

They are a fat 13-point underdog and they will hear for the next two weeks how they are heading into Mission Impossible trying to keep the Patriots from a historical 19-0 season and perfection.

"The Patriots are a good football team, it's going to be a fight, we're going to go in there and give 'em our best," running back Brandon Jacobs said.

"We went against every quarterback, everybody say you can't beat that guy," linebacker Antonio Pierce said.

"You can't beat Jeff Garcia, you can't beat Tony Romo, you can't beat Brett Favre in the cold weather."

And now, you can't beat Tom Brady.

"That's beautiful," Pierce said. "That's what we want." ■

Plaxico Burress makes the winning catch for the go-ahead touchdown with 35 seconds left in the game.

Super Bowl XLII • February 3, 2008
Giants 17 • Patriots 14

Giant Piece Of History

MVP Performance Is One For The Ages By Paul Schwartz

The imperfect team picked the perfect time to deny perfection. There was 2:39 remaining last night in Super Bowl XLII and the Giants had fought the good fight, the gallant fight but after all their pummeling of Tom Brady and inspired play they were trailing 14-10 after Brady's touchdown pass to Randy Moss seemed to finally save the Patriots and send the Giant home as lovable losers.

As Eli Manning stepped onto the grass one last time at University of Phoenix Stadium, all along the Giants sideline players were keeping the faith, nearly chanting in unison. "I was thinking about an Eli Manning great comeback," defensive end Justin Tuck said. "We were running up and down the sideline yelling 'Believe'."

Michael Strahan needed more. He screamed, over and over, "17-14!" demanding all within earshot buy in. "I said 'Believe it . . . don't just say it, believe it'!"

In the huddle, Manning barely raised his voice.

"We're going to go down and score," he stated.

"We believed in him," guard Chris Snee said. Perhaps that is why they won.

"I'll tell you what," co-owner John Mara said. "It's the greatest victory in the history of this franchise, without question."

Completing an astonishing season with a game for the ages, the Giants shocked the world, denied history and defeated the Patriots 17-14 in a remarkable Super Bowl XLII stunner. Manning's 13-yard pass to a wide-open Plaxico Burress – who ran past a stumbling cornerback, Ellis Hobbs – with 35 seconds left set the final dagger in one of the greatest contests and upsets in Super Bowl history. Manning directed a 12- play, 83-yard drive – kept alive by a miracle Manning escape and 32-yard pass to a skywalking David Tyree – to outduel the usually immaculate Brady to win the MVP awar that his big brother Peyton won one year ago with the Colts.

"Every team is beatable," said Tom Coughlin, the jubilant comeback coach. "The right moment, the right time, every team is beatable." What was supposed to be the coronation of the Patriots' immaculate 19-0 season instead became one of the most unexpected defeats in this game's storied history. The Pats sought to copyright the 19-0 trademark; instead, they'd better get busy printing up those "18-1" shirts.

"It's unbelievable," Eli Manning said. "It's the fight of this team."

There was no time for the battered Brady to stage a comeback and when rookie Jay Alford dropped Brady for the Giants fifth sack and two more desperation passes fell incomplete, Manning took a final knee and the Giants erupted in celebration.

"They were so relaxed at the end when we were driving down it was unbelievable, like ho-hum, they're going

David Tyree is congratulated by teammates after his fourth quarter touchdown catch.

Michael Strahan and the Giants defensive line harassed and hounded Tom Brady and the Patriots all game, including this soaring second-quarter sack.

to give it to us and we didn't give them anything," said receiver Amani Toomer, a champion after 12 seasons with the Giants. "During the drive [defensive end] Richard Seymour said to us 'Get ready to go home guys.' I don't care what they say, they were expecting us to crack. We're a tough team in a tough city and that's what we represent."

That city will open its arms and hearts to the Giants tomorrow will a ticker-tape parade. "They moved the parade from Boston to New York City!" exclaimed Strahan, who came back for a 15th season and soon will be fitted for a championship ring.

"We shocked the world," Antonio Pierce said. "But not ourselves."

The Giants (14-6) won their record 11th consecutive non-home game after trailing in the final minute, only the

R.W. McQuarters and his teammates celebrate after winning Super Bowl XLII.

second time that has happened in the 42-year history of the Super Bowl. They deserved everything they got, often dominating with an always fearsome, relentless defensive posse that limited the most prolific offense in NFL history to 274 total yards.

Burress last week boldly predicted to *The Post* that the Giants would win 23-17 and he actually shortchanged his defensive teammates. "I opened my big mouth last week, Burress said. "I put a little pressure on the defense; if it wasn't for the defense we wouldn't have even been in the game."

Never did the Giants look in awe. They took a 3-0 lead with a opening drive of nearly 10 minutes but were waste-

Ahmad Bradshaw runs the ball passed the Pats Ty Warren (94) and Mike Vrabel (50) in the second quarter.

ful in the red zone and trailed 7-3 at halftime. That's the way it stood after three quarters, with Strahan and Tuck and Osi Umenyiora applying lethal pressure on Brady, dealing with Moss but barely slowing Wes Welker.

On the first play of the fourth quarter, Manning found rookie tight end Kevin Boss on a 45-yard catch-and-run, hit rookie Steve Smith for 17 more and finally found Tyree—who did not have a scoring catch all season—on a strike over the middle for a 5-yard touchdown pass. With 11:05 remaining th Giants led 10-7.

The proud Patriots responded. Brady drove them 80 yards and when cornerback Corey Webster slipped, Moss had an easy 6-yard scoring catch with 2:42 to go. Perfection was there for the taking, but Manning had other ideas. Manning hit Toomer for 11 yards. Brandon Jacobs on fourth down picked up the first down. And

then, on third-and-5, Manning was all-but sacked, in the clutches of Seymour and Jarvis Green and the Giants were finished. "I don't know how he got out of there," Seymour said.

No one knew, but he did, escaping and floating a pass that Tyree had no business catching, but he did, out-leaping Rodney Harrison on the New England 24. A sideline pass to Smith set up the play heard around the world, as Burress made Hobbs and the Patriots pay for defending him with one player.

"Nobody thought we could do it," an emotional Toomer said.

They did it. ∎

After a desperate Eli Manning scramble, David Tyree's 32-yard circus catch off his helmet while in the clutches of Patriots safety Rodney Harrison was the signature play of the game.

SuperMann By Steve Serby

Eli Manning will never be more perfect for New York than he was last night, when he was SuperMann, when he stood eyeball-to-eyeball with the great Tom Brady and shot him dead with the whole world watching.

He gave us the perfect drive at the perfect time, and smashed Bill Belichick's perfect season to smithereens, and brought the Lombardi Trophy home to us. Giants 17, Patriots 14. Perfect upset. Perfect ending.

Manning was better when it counted than Tony Romo, better in the arctic cold than Brett Favre . . . better than Brady when his franchise asked him to go win its third Super Bowl.

You bet he wanted that game in his hands at the end.

"You want a shot to win the game at the end," MVP-li said. "As a quarterback, that's all you want."

You bet the Giants, and his own family, wanted the ball in his hands at the end.

"As a quarterback, I've had an appreciation for Eli's ability to remain calm in the highest pressure situations," big brother Peyton Manning said. "The best quarterbacks are able to win in those moments as opposed to being overwhelmed by them."

Manning had risen up and given the Giants a 10-7 lead when he found David Tyree with a 5-yard TD pass.

But Brady had it back at his 20 with 7:54 left.

And this is when he finally began looking like Brady, surgicall dissecting Big Blue until he looked right for Randy Moss. Corey Webster slipped and fell. Touchdown. Pats 14, Giants 10. Peyton peered at the television.

"You can't really see his exact facial expression, but you could see his body language, and he was just calm; it wasn't a panic, it was, 'Hey, we got 2:45 to go, we got some timeouts, we'll have the ball last, let's go make it happen," Peyton said. "That's the best characteristic a quarterback can have and nobody does it better than Eli."

Eli had it at his 17 with 2:39 left and three timeouts left.

"This is where you want to be," MVP-li said in the huddle. "Let's go win the game."

On third-and-10 from the 28, he hit Amani Toomer for nine. Fourth-and-season. Brandon Jacobs got the yard.

Now Eli somehow, some way, escaped the clutches of Jarvis Green and Richard Seymour, spun away to his right, heaved one down the middle for David Tyree, one of the more unlikely Super Bowl heroes you will find.

"I'm kinda looking forward to getting home and seeing it on TV – I Tivo'd on Direct TV," Manning said.

Tyree leaped alongside Rodney Harrison, the ball resting tantalizingly on Tyree's helmet. Tyree somehow had the presence of mind to keep both hands gripped on the ball and a 32-yard gain.

"You'd be hard-pressed to find a play that would be as great a play in Super Bowl history, in my opinion," Peyton said.

It all started with Eli's escape.

"No one pulled me down," he said. "Saw a little lane, tried to get through there, was able to squeeze through, looked downfield, saw David Tyree, threw the ball up, and it was really an unbelievable catch by him."

Eli, third-and-11 now at the Patriot 24.

He found Steve Smith by the right sidelines for 12 yards. Out of bounds.

Thirty-nine seconds to the Lombardi Trophy. No timeouts left.

Belichick blitzed. Single coverage. A fade. Plaxico Burress, questionable with a knee and an ankle, ran right past Ellis Hobbs. And Manning found him in the left corner of the end zone with 35 seconds left, and Big Blue wasn't letting Brady get his fourth ring, no way.

"It came down to one play and we made it," said Burress, so close on his

AP/Wide World

23-17 prediction.

"I gave the guy a move, and Eli put it up."

And his mother Olivia and fiancée Abby shared some tears.

"I was just glad the ball was in his hands at the end of the game with a chance to win it as opposed to Brady," Peyton said.

Manning out-Bradyed Tom Brady, that's all he did. And found himself a place in New York sports lore along-side Broadway Joe and Phil Simms.

When a final Brady prayer for Moss fell incomplete, the pro-Giants stadium erupted. The Giants bench erupted.

For most of the night, Big Blue had saved MVP-li, knocking Brady from one end of University of Phoenix Stadium to the next, because defensive coordinator Steve Spagnuolo was the young Belichick.

Now Belichick can kiss that aster-isk goodbye. Thanks to MV-Pli. SuperMann.

In the locker room, Eli bent down to congratulate Lt. Col. Greg Gadson, the Giants' inspiration. "We did it," Eli said.

Peyton came over and the brothers shared a Super moment together by MVP-li's locker.

"I'm just as excited as every Giant fan in the country," proud papa Archie said. ■

New York Giants defensive end Osi Umenyiora pressures New England Patriots quarterback Tom Brady in the third quarter.

Team Stats

	1	2	3	4	Final
NY Giants	3	0	0	14	17
New England	0	7	0	7	14

	Giants	Patriots
First Downs	17	22
Passing	13	17
Rushing	4	3
Penalty	0	2
Third Down Efficiency	8-16	7-14
Fourth Down Efficiency	1-1	0-2
TOTAL NET YARDS	338	274
Total Plays	63	69
Average Gain Per Play	5.4	4.0
NET YARDS RUSHING	91	45
Rushes	26	16
Average Per Rush	3.5	2.8
NET YARDS PASSING	247	229
Completions-Attempts	19-34	29-48
Yards Per Pass Play	6.7	4.3
Times Sacked	3	5
Yards Lost to Sacks	8	37
Had Intercepted	1	0
PUNTS	4	4
Average Punt	39.0	43.8
PENALTIES	4	5
Penalty Yards	36	35
FUMBLES	2	1
Fumbles Lost	0	1
TIME OF POSSESSION	30:27	29:33

Eli Manning celebrates after the Giants win the Super Bowl.